LIKE CHRIST

Andrew Murray

Publisher's Note

So that Andrew Murray's inspiring message may be presented in an understandable manner to the twentieth century reader, we have updated both the language and the sentence structure of the nineteenth century edition. It is a joy to be able to share this book, so that all who read it may go on to become *Like Christ.*

LIKE CHRIST

Printed in the United States of America
ISBN: 0-88368-122-6

CONTENTS

PREFACE

In presenting this book on the image of our blessed Lord, and the likeness to Him to which we are called, I have only two remarks to make.

The one is that no one can be more conscious than myself of the difficulty of the task which I have undertaken, and the defectiveness of its execution. There were two things I had to do. The one was to draw such a portrait of the Son of God, as "in all things...made like unto His brethren" (Hebrews 2:17), in order to show how, in the reality of His human life, He was an exact pattern of what the Father wants us to be. I wanted to offer a portrait that would make likeness to Him infinitely and mightily attractive, arouse desire, awaken love, inspire hope, and strengthen faith in all who are seeking to imitate Jesus Christ. And then, I had to sketch another portrait—that of the believer as he really, with some degree of spiritual exactness, reflects this image. And, one that, amid the trials and duties of daily life, would prove that likeness to Christ is no mere ideal, but, through the power of the Holy Spirit, a most blessed reality.

How often and how deeply I have felt, after trying to explain one trait of the blessed life, how utterly insufficient human thoughts are to grasp, or human words to express, that spiritual beauty which one can at best see only faint glimpses. And, how often our very thoughts deceive us as they give us some human conception of what the Word reveals, while we lack that true vision of the spiritual glory of Him who is the brightness of the Father's glory.

The second remark I wish to make is a suggestion as to what I think is truly needed to behold the glory of the blessed image into which we are to be changed. I was very much struck some time ago by the practice a class in object lessons was put through. A picture was shown them, which they were told to look at carefully. They then had to shut their eyes, and take time to think and remember everything they had seen. The picture was now removed, and the students had to tell everything they could remember. Again, they were shown the picture, and they had to try and notice what they had not observed before. Again, they had to shut their eyes, think and then tell what more they had noticed. And so once more, until every line of the picture had been taken in. As I looked at the keen interest with which the little eyes now gazed on the picture, and then were pressed so tightly shut as they tried to realize, take in, and keep what they had been looking at, I felt that if our Bible reading were more of such an object-lesson, the unseen spiritual realities pictured to us in the Word would take much deeper hold of our inner life.

We are too easily content with the thoughts suggested by the words of the Bible instead of giving time for the substantial, spiritual reality, which the Word as the truth of God contains, to be lodged and rooted in the heart. Let us, in meditating on the image of God in Christ, to which we are to be conformed, remember this. When some special trait has occupied our thoughts, let us shut our eyes, and open our hearts. Let us think, pray, and believe in the working of the Holy Spirit, until we really see the blessed Master in that special light in which the Word has been setting Him before us. Let us carry away for that day the deep and abiding impression of that heavenly beauty in Him which we know is to be reproduced in us. Let us gaze, and gaze again; let us worship and adore. The more we see Him as He is, the more like Him we must become. Study the image of God in the man Christ Jesus, yield and open your innermost being for that image to take possession and live in you, and then go forth and let the heavenly likeness reflect itself and shine out in your life among your fellow-men. This is what we have been redeemed for; let this be what we live for.

And now, I intrust this book to the gracious care of the blessed Lord of whose glory it seeks to tell. May He let us see that there is no beauty or blessedness like that of a Christlike life. May He teach us to believe that, in union with Him, the Christlike life is indeed for us. And, as each day we listen to what His Word tells us of His image, may each one of us have grace to say, "O my Father! even as Your beloved Son lived in You, with You, for You on earth, even so would I also live."

Andrew Murray
Wellington, Cape of Good Hope.

P.S. As the tone of the meditations is mostly personal, I have, at the end of the volume, added some more general thoughts: "On Preaching Christ as our Example."

Chapter 1

LIKE CHRIST...
Because We Abide In Him

"He that saith he abideth in him ought himself also to walk, even as he walked"—1 John 2:6.

Abiding in Christ and walking like Christ: these two blessings of the new life are presented here in their essential unity. The fruit of a life *in Christ* is a life *like Christ.*

To the first of these expressions, *abiding in Christ,* we are no strangers. The wondrous parable of the Vine and the branches, with the accompanying command, "Abide in Me, and I in you" (John 15:4), has often been a source of rich instruction and comfort. And though we feel as if we have only imperfectly learned the lesson of abiding in Him, yet we have tasted something of the joy that comes when the soul can say: Lord, You know all things. You know that I do abide in You. And, He also knows how often the fervent prayer still arises: Blessed Lord, do grant me the complete, unbroken abiding.

The second expression, *walking like Christ,* is no less significant than the first. It is the promise of the wonderful power which abiding in Him will exert. As the fruit of our surrender to live wholly in Him, His life works so mightily in us that our walk—the outward expression of the inner life—becomes like His. The two are inseparably connected. The *abiding in* always precedes the *walking like* Him. And yet, the desire to walk like Him must equally precede any large amount of abiding. Only then is the need for a close union fully realized. The heavenly Giver is free to bestow the fullness of His grace, because He sees that the soul is prepared to use it according to His design. When the Savior said, "If ye keep My commandments, ye shall abide in My love" (John 15:10), He meant this: the surrender to walk like Me is the path to the full abiding in Me. Many will discover that this is the secret of his failure in abiding in Christ—he did not seek it with the idea of walking like Christ. The words of John invite us to look at the two truths in their vital connection and dependence on each other.

The first lesson they teach is: He who seeks to abide in Christ *must walk even as He walked.* We all know that it is a matter of course that a branch bear fruit of the same sort as the vine to which it belongs. The life of the vine and the branch is so completely identical that the manifestation of that life must be identical, too. When the Lord Jesus redeemed us with His blood, and presented us to the Father in His righteousness, He did not leave us in our old nature to serve God as best we could. No, in Him dwelt the eternal life—the holy, divine life of heaven—and everyone who is in Him receives that same eternal life in its holy, heavenly power. Hence, nothing can be more natural than the claim that he who abides in Him, continually receiving life from Him, must *also so* walk *even as He* walked.

This mighty life of God in the soul does not, however, work as a blind force compelling us ignorantly or involuntarily to act like Christ. On the contrary, the walking like Him must be the result of a deliberate choice—sought in strong desire, accepted by a living will. With this view, the Father in heaven showed us, in Jesus' earthly life, what the life of heaven would be when it came down into the conditions and circumstances of our human life. And, with the same object, the Lord Jesus—when we receive the new life from Him, and when He calls us to abide in Him so that we may receive that life more abundantly—points us to His own life on earth. He tells us that the new life has been bestowed so that we may walk even as He walked. "Even as I, so ye also." That word of the Master takes His whole earthly life, and very simply makes it the rule and guide of all our conduct. If we abide in Jesus, we may not act other than He did. "Like Christ" gives, in one short, all-inclusive word, the blessed law of the Christian life. He is to think, to speak, to act as Jesus did; as Jesus was, *even so* he is to be.

The second lesson is the complement of the first: He who seeks to walk like Christ, *must abide in Him.*

There is a twofold need of this lesson. With some, there is the earnest desire and effort to follow

Christ's example. And yet, they have no sense of how impossible it is to do so without a deep, real abiding in Him. They fail because they seek to obey the high command to live like Christ, without the only power that can do so—the living *in* Christ. With others, there is the opposite error. They know their own weakness, and think that walking like Christ is an impossibility. Those who seek to do it and who fail need the lesson as much as those who do not seek because they expect to fail. To walk like Christ one must abide in Him. He who abides in Him has the power to walk like Him; not in himself or his own efforts, but in Jesus, who perfects His strength in our weakness.

It is when I feel my utter weakness most deeply, and fully accept Jesus in His wondrous union to myself as my life, that His power works in me. Then, I am able to lead a life completely beyond what my own power could obtain. I begin to see that abiding in Him is not a matter of moments or special seasons, but the deep life process in which—by His keeping grace—I continue without a moment's intermission, and from which I act out all my Christian life. And, I feel encouraged to really take Him as my entire example, because I am sure that the hidden, inner union and likeness must work itself out into a visible likeness in walk and conduct.

Dear reader! if God gives us grace, in the course of our meditations, to truly enter into the meaning of His words and what they teach about a life like Christ's, we will more than once come into contact with the heights and depths that will make us cry out, "How can these things be?" If the Holy Spirit reveals the heavenly perfection of the humanity of our Lord as the image of the unseen God, and speaks, "*so, even so* ought ye also to walk," the first effect will be that we will begin to feel how far we are from Him. We will be ready to give up hope, and to say with so many, "There's no reason to even try, I can never walk like Jesus." At such moments, we will find our strength in the message, *He that abideth in Him, he* must, *he* can, also walk even as He walked. The word of the Master will come with new meaning as the assurance of sufficient strength. He who abides in Me bears much fruit.

Therefore, brethren, abide in Him! Every believer is in Christ. But, everyone does not abide in Him in the consciously joyful and trustful surrender of their whole being given up to His influence. You know what abiding in Him is. It is to consent with our whole soul to His being our life, to depend on Him to inspire us in all that goes to make up life, and then to absolutely give up everything so that He may rule and work in us. It is resting in the full assurance that He does, each moment, work in us what we are to be. He Himself enables us to maintain that perfect surrender, in which He is free to do all His will.

Let all who do indeed long to walk like Christ find courage in the thought of what He is and will prove Himself to be if they trust Him. He is the *true Vine*; no vine ever did so fully for its branches what He will do for us. We only have to consent to be branches.

Honor Him by a joyful trust that He is, beyond all conception, the *true Vine*, holding you by His almighty strength, supplying you from His infinite fullness. And, as your faith thus looks to Him, instead of sighing and failure, the voice of praise will be heard repeating the language of faith: Thanks be to God! he who abides in Him does walk even as He walked. Thanks be to God! I abide in Him, and I walk as He walked. Yes, thanks be to God! In the blessed life of God's redeemed, these two are inseparably one: abiding in Christ and walking like Christ.

Blessed Savior! You know how often I have said, Lord, I do abide in You! And yet, I sometimes feel that the full joy and power of a life in You is lacking. Your word this day has reminded me of what the reason for my failure might be. I sought to abide in You more for my own comfort and growth than for Your glory. I did not fully understand how the hidden union with You had for its object perfect conformity to You. I didn't realize how only he who wholly yields himself to serve and obey the Father as completely as You did can fully receive all that the heavenly love can do for him. I now see something of it: the entire surrender to live and work like You must precede the full experience of the wondrous power of Your life.

Lord, I thank You for the discovery. With my whole heart I accept Your calling, and yield myself in everything to walk *even as* You walked. To be

Your faithful follower in all that You were and did on earth is the one desire of my heart.

Blessed Lord! he who truly yields himself to walk as You walked, will receive grace to wholly abide in You. O my Lord! here I am. *To walk like Christ!* for this I do indeed consecrate myself to You. *To abide in Christ!* for this I trust in You with full assurance of faith. Perfect in me Your own work.

And, let the Holy Spirit help me, O my Lord! each time I meditate on what it is to walk like You, to hold fast the blessed truth: as one who abides *in Christ,* I have the strength to walk *like Christ.* Amen.

Chapter 2

LIKE CHRIST...
He Himself Calls Us

"I have given you an example, that ye should do, as I have done to you"—John 13:15.

It is Jesus Christ, the beloved Redeemer of our souls, who speaks thus. He had just humbled Himself to do the work of the slave by washing His disciples' feet. In doing so, His love demonstrated to the body the service which was lacking at the supper table. At the same time, He showed, in a striking symbol, what He had done for their souls in cleansing them from sin. In this twofold work of love, He set before them, just before parting, in one significant act, the whole work of His life as a ministry of blessing to body *and* soul. And as He sits down, He says: *"I have given you an example, that ye should do, as I have done to you."* All that they had seen in Him and experienced from Him is thus made the rule of their life: "Even as I have done, do also."

The word of the blessed Savior applies to us, too. To each one who knows that the Lord has washed away his sin, He commands with all the touching force of one who is going out to die, "Even as I have done to you, so do ye also." Jesus Christ does indeed ask everyone of us in everything to act just as we have seen Him do. What He has done to us, and still does each day, we are to do over again to others. In His condescending, pardoning, saving love, He is our example; each of us is to be the copy and image of the Master.

At once, we think, "Alas! how seldom I have lived like Christ. How little I have even known that I was expected to live thus!" And yet, He is my Lord; He loves me, and I love Him. I must not entertain the thought of living in any other way than He would have me. I must open my heart to His Word, and fix my gaze on His example, until it exercises its divine power upon me, and draws me with irresistible force to cry: Lord, even as You have done, so will I do also.

The power of an example mainly depends on two things. The one is its attractiveness, the other is the personal relationship and influence of him in whom the example is seen. In both aspects, what power there is in our Lord's example!

Or, is there really anything very attractive in our Lord's example? I ask it in all earnestness, because, judging from the conduct of many of His disciples, it would really seem as if it were not so. O that the Spirit of God would open our eyes to see the heavenly beauty of the likeness of the only-begotten Son!

We know who the Lord Jesus is. He is the Son of the all-glorious God, one with the Father in nature and glory and perfection. When He had been on earth, it could be said of Him, "We show you that eternal life, which was with the Father, was manifested unto us." In Him, we see God. In Him, we see how God would act were He here in our place on earth. In Him, all that is beautiful and lovely and perfect in the heavenly world is revealed to us in the form of an earthly life. If we want to see what is really considered to be noble and glorious in the heavenly world, if we want to see what is really divine, we have only to look at Jesus. In all He does, the glory of God is shown forth.

But oh, the blindness of God's children: this heavenly beauty is not attractive to many of them. They see no reason to desire it.

The manner and way of living in the court of an earthly king greatly influence the ways of the empire over which he rules. The example it gives is imitated by all who belong to the nobility or the higher classes. But, the example of the King of heaven—who came and dwelt in the flesh, that we might see how we here on earth might live a Godlike life—is rarely imitated by His followers. When we look upon Jesus, His obedience to the will of the Father, His humiliaton to be a servant of the most unworthy, His love as manifested in the entire giving up and sacrifice of Himself, we see the most wondrous and glorious thing heaven has to show. In heaven itself, we will see nothing greater or brighter. Surely such an example, given by God with the intention of making the imitation attractive and possible, ought to win us. Is it not enough to stir all that is within us with a holy jealousy and with joy unutterable as we hear the message, "I have given you an example, that ye should do as I have done to you"?

This is not all. The power of an example consists not only in its own intrinsic excellence, but also in the personal relationship to him who gives it. Jesus had not washed the feet of others in the presence of His disciples. It was when He had washed *their feet* that He said: "Ye should do as I have done to you" (John 13:15). It is the consciousness of a personal relationship to Christ that enforces the command: Do as I have done. It is the experience of what Jesus has done to me that is the strength in which I can go and do the same to others. He does not ask that I do more than has been done to me. But, He does not expect less either: Even as I have done to you. He does not ask that I humble myself as a servant deeper than He has done. It would not have been strange if He had asked this of such a worm. But this is not His wish. He only demands that I do and be what He, the King, has done and been.

He humbled Himself as low as humiliation could go, to love and to bless me. He counted this *His highest honor and blessedness.* And now, He invites me to partake of the same honor and blessedness, in loving and serving as He did. Truly, if I indeed know the love that rests on me, the humiliation through which alone that love could reach me, and the power of the cleansing which has washed me, nothing can stop me from saying: "Yes, blessed Lord, even as You have done to me, I will also do." The heavenly loveliness of the great Example, and the divine lovingness of the great Exemplar are combined to make His example more attractive than anything else.

There is only one thing I must not forget. It is not the remembrance of what Jesus has once done to me, but the living experience of what He is now to me, that will give me the power to act like Him. His love must be a present reality—the inflowing of a life and a power in which I can love like Him. It is only through the Holy Spirit that I can realize what Jesus is doing for me, how He does it, that it is He who does it, and that it is possible for me to do to others what He is doing to me.

"Even as I have done to you, do ye also!" What a precious word! What a glorious prospect! Jesus is going to show forth in me the divine power of His love, so that I may show it forth to others. He blesses me, that I may bless others. He loves me, that I may love others. He becomes a servant to me, that I may become a servant to others. He saves and cleanses me, that I may save and cleanse others. He gives Himself wholly for and to me, that I may wholly give myself for and to others. I have only to be doing to others what He is doing to me—nothing more. I can do it, *because* He is doing it to me. What I do is nothing but repeating, showing forth, what I am receiving from Him. (See Numbers 10:32.)

Wondrous grace! which thus calls us to be like our

Lord in that which constitutes His highest glory. Wondrous grace! which fits us for this calling by Himself first being to us and in us what we are to be to others. Our whole heart will joyously respond to His command. Yes, blessed Lord! even as You do to me will I also do to others.

Gracious Lord! what can I now do but praise and pray? My heart feels overwhelmed with this wondrous offer: that You will reveal all Your love and power in me if I will yield myself to let it flow through me to others. Though with fear and trembling, yet in deep, grateful adoration, with joy and confidence, I accept the offer and say: Here I am. Show me how much You love me, and I will show it to others by loving them even so.

And that I may be able to do this, blessed Lord, grant me these two things. Grant me, by Your Holy Spirit, a clear insight into Your love for me, that I may know how You love me, how Your love for me is Your delight and blessedness, how in that love You give Yourself so completely to me, that You are indeed mine to do for me all I need. Grant this, Lord, and I will know how to love and live for others, even as You love and live for me.

And then grant me to see, as often as I feel how little love I have, that it is not with the love of my little heart, but with Your love shed abroad in me, that I have to fulfill the command of loving like You. Am I not Your branch, O my heavenly Vine? It is the fullness of Your life and love that flows through me in love and blessing to those around. It is Your Spirit that, at the same moment, reveals what You are to me, and strengthens me for what I am to be to others in Your name. In this faith, I dare to say, Amen, Lord, even as You do to me, I also do. Yes, Amen.

Chapter 3

LIKE CHRIST...
As One That Serves

"If I then, your Lord and Master, have washed your feet; ye also ought to wash one another's feet"—John 13:14.

"I am among you as he that serveth"—Luke 22:27.

In the last chapter, we spoke of the Lord's right to demand and expect that His redeemed ones follow His example. Now, we will more deeply consider in what it is we have to follow Him.

"Ye also ought to wash one another's feet" is the word which we want to fully understand. The *form* of a servant in which we see Him, the *cleansing* which was the object of *that* service, the *love* which was its motive power, these are the three main thoughts.

First, the *form* of a servant. All was ready for the last supper, down to the very water to wash the feet of the guests, according to custom. But, there was no slave to do the work. Each one waited for the other: none of the twelve thought of humbling himself to do the work. Even at the table, they were concerned with who should be greatest in the Kingdom they were expecting (Luke 22:26,27). All at once, Jesus rises (they were still sitting at the table), lays aside His garments, girds Himself with a towel, and begins to wash their feet. O wondrous spectacle! on which angels gazed with adoring wonder. Christ, the Creator and King of the universe, at whose beck legions of angels are ready to serve Him, might have said, lovingly, which one of the twelve must do the work. But, Christ chooses the slave's place for His own, takes the soiled feet in His own holy hands, and washes them. He does it in full consciousness of His divine glory, for John says, "Jesus knowing that the Father had given all things into His hands, and that He was come from God, and went to God, rose" (John 13:3). For the hands into which God had given all things, nothing is common or unclean. The lowliness of a work never lowers the person. The person honors and elevates the work, and imparts his own worth even to the most meager of service.

In such deep humiliation, as we men call it, our Lord finds divine glory, and is in this the Leader of His Church in the path of true blessedness. It is as the Son that He is the servant. Just because He is the beloved of His Father, in whose hands all things are given, it is not difficult for Him to stoop so low. In thus taking the form of a servant, Jesus proclaims the law of rank in the Church of Christ. The higher one wishes to stand in grace, the more it must be his joy to be the servant of all. "Whosoever will be chief among you, let him be your servant" (Matthew

20:27); "He that is greatest among you shall be your servant" (Matthew 23:11). The higher I rise in the consciousness of being like Christ, God's beloved child, the deeper I will stoop to serve all around me.

A servant is one who is always caring for the work and interest of his master. He is ever ready to let his master see that he only seeks to do what will please or profit him. Thus Jesus lived: "For even the Son of man came not to be ministered unto, but to minister, and to give His life a ransom for many" (Mark 10:45); "I am among you as He that serveth." Thus I must live, moving among God's children as the servant of all. If I seek to bless others, it must be in the humble, loving readiness with which I serve them, not caring for my own honor or interest, but only to be a blessing to them. I must follow Christ's example in washing the disciples' feet. A servant is not ashamed or humiliated by being regarded as an inferior: it is his place and work to serve others. The reason why we so often do not bless others is because we want to show that we are superior to them in grace or gifts, or at last their equals. If only we would learn from our Lord how to associate with others in the blessed spirit of a servant, what a blessing we would become to the world! Once this example is restored to the place it ought to have in the Church of Christ, the power of His presence will soon make itself known.

And now, what work is the disciple supposed to perform in this spirit of lowly service? The foot washing speaks of a double work—for the cleansing and refreshing of the body, and for the saving of the soul. During the whole of our Lord's life on earth, these two things were ever united: "The sick were healed, to the poor the gospel was preached" (see Luke 7:22). As with the paralytic and many others, blessing to the body was the type and promise of a life given up to the Spirit.

The follower of Jesus may not lose sight of this when he receives the command, "Ye also ought to wash one another's feet" (John 13:14). Remembering that the external and bodily is the gate to the inner and spiritual life, he makes the salvation of the soul the first object in his holy ministry of love. At the same time, however, he seeks the way to the hearts of the people by the ready service of love in the little and common things of daily life. It is not by reproof and scolding that he shows that he is a servant. No, it is by the friendliness and kindliness with which he proves, in daily activity, that he is always thinking about how he can help or serve. He thus becomes the living witness of what it is to be a follower of Jesus. From someone such as this, the word, when spoken, comes with power and finds easy entrance into the hearts of those who listen. And then, when he comes in contact with the sin, perverseness, and contradiction of men, instead of being discouraged, he perseveres because he knows how much patience Jesus has borne with him, and still daily cleanses him. He realizes himself to be one of God's appointed servants, to stoop to the lowest depth to serve and save men, even to bow at the feet of others if this be needed.

The spirit which will enable one to live such a life of loving service can be learned from Jesus alone. John writes, "Having loved His own which were in the world, He loved them to the end" (John 13:1). For love, nothing is too hard. Love never speaks of sacrifice. To bless the loved one, however unworthy, it willingly gives up all. It was love that made Jesus a servant. It is love alone that will make the servant's place and work such blessedness to us that we will persevere in it at all costs. We may perhaps, like Jesus, have to wash the feet of some Judas who rewards us with ingratitude and betrayal. We will probably meet many a Peter, who at first, with his "Never my feet" refuses, and is then dissatisfied when we do not comply with his impatient "Not my feet only, but also my hands and my head" (John 13:9). Only love, a heavenly unquenchable love, gives the patience, the courage, and the wisdom for this great work the Lord has set before us in His holy example: "Wash ye one another's feet."

Try, above all, to understand that it is only as a son that you can truly be a servant. It was as the Son that Christ took the form of a servant. In this, you will find the secret of willing, happy service. Walk among men *as a Son of the most high God.* A Son of God is only in the world to show forth His Father's glory, and to prove how Godlike and blessed it is to live only and at any cost to find a way to offer love to the hearts of the lost.

O my soul, your love cannot attain to this. Therefore, listen to Him who says, "Abide in *My love.*" Our one desire must be that He may show us how He loves us, and that He Himself may keep us abiding in "*His love.*" Live every day as the beloved of the Lord, in the experience that His love washes, cleanses, bears, and blesses you all the day long. His love flowing into you will flow out again from you, and make it your greatest joy to follow His example in washing the feet of others.

Do not complain about the lack of love and humility in others, but pray much that the Lord would awaken His people to their calling. Pray that they would follow in His footsteps, that the world may see that they have taken Him for their example. And, if you do not see it as soon as you wish in those around you, let it only urge you to more earnest prayer. In you, at least, the Lord may have one who understands and proves that to love and serve like Jesus is the highest blessedness and joy, as well as the way, like Jesus, to be a blessing and a joy to others.

My Lord, I give myself to You to live this blessed life of service. In You, I have seen it—the spirit of a servant is a kingly spirit, come from heaven and lifting up to heaven, the Spirit of God's own Son. Your everlasting love, dwell in me, and my life will be like Yours, and the language of my life to others as Yours, "I am in the midst of you as He that serveth."

O glorified Son of God, You know how little of Your Spirit dwells in us, how this life of a servant is opposed to all that the world deems honorable or proper. But, You have come to teach us new lessons of what is right, to show us what is thought in heaven of the glory of being the least, of the blessedness of serving. O You who not only gives new thoughts, but implants new feelings, give me a heart like Yours, a heart full of the Holy Spirit, a heart that can love as You did. O Lord, Your Holy Spirit dwells within me. Your fullness is my inheritance; in the joy of the Holy Spirit, I can be as You are. I do yield myself to a life of service like Yours. Let the same mind be in me which was also in You when You made Yourself of no reputation, took upon You the form of a servant, and, being found in fashion as a man, humbled Yourself. Yes, Lord, that very same mind be in me, too, by Your grace. As a son of God, let me be the servant of men. Amen.

Chapter 4

LIKE CHRIST . . .
Our Head

"For even hereunto were ye called: because Christ also suffered for us, leaving us an example, that ye should follow his steps....who his own self bare our sins in his own body on the tree, that we, being dead to sins, should live unto righteousness"—1 Peter 2:21-24.

The call to follow Christ's example and to walk in His footsteps is so high that there is every reason to wonder, How can sinful men be expected to walk like the Son of God? The answer that most people give is practical —it cannot really be expected. The command sets before us an ideal, beautiful but unattainable.

The answer Scripture gives is different. It points us to the wonderful relationship in which we stand to Christ. Because our union to Him stirs within us a heavenly life with all its powers, the claim that we should live as Christ did may be made in downright earnest. The realization of this relationship between Christ and His people is necessary for everyone who is serious in following Christ's example.

And what is this relationship? It is threefold. Peter speaks in this passage of Christ as our *Surety,* our *Example,* and our *Head.*

Christ is our *Surety.* "Christ also suffered for *us";* "Who His own self *bare our sins* in His own body on the tree" (1 Peter 2:21,24). As Surety, Christ suffered and died in our *stead.* He bore our sin, and at once broke its curse and power. As Surety, He did what we could not do, what we now need not do.

Christ is also our *Example.* In one sense, His work is unique. In another, we have to follow Him in it; we must do as He did, live and suffer like Him. "Christ also *suffered for us, leaving us an Example,* that ye should follow His steps" (1 Peter 2:21). His suffering as my Surety calls me to a suffering like His as my Example. But is this reasonable? In His sufferings as Surety, He had the power of the divine nature, and how can I be expected in the weakness of the flesh to suffer as He did? Is there not an impassable gulf between these two things which Peter unites so closely, the suffering as Surety and the suffering as Example? No, there is a blessed third aspect of Christ's work which bridges that gulf, which is the connecting link between Christ as Surety and Christ as Example, which makes it possible for us in very deed to take the Surety as Example, and live, suffer, and die like Him.

Christ is also our *Head.* In this, His Suretyship and His Example have their root and unity. Christ is the second Adam. As a believer, I am spiritually one with Him. In this union, He lives in me, and imparts to me, the power of His finished work, the power of His sufferings and death and resurrection. It is on this ground that we are taught, in Romans 6 and elsewhere, that the Christian is indeed dead to sin and alive to God. The very life that Christ lives—the life that passed through death and the power of that death—works in the believer. Thus, he is dead, and has risen again with Christ. It is this thought that Peter utters when he says: "Who His own self bore our sins upon the tree," not only that we, through His death, might receive forgiveness, but "that we, being *dead to sins, should live* unto righteousness."

As we have part in the spiritual death of the first Adam, having really died to God in him, so we have part in the second Adam, having really died to sin in Him. In Him, we are made alive again to God. Christ is not only our Surety who lived and died for us, our Example who showed us how to live and die, but also our Head, with whom we are one, in whose death we have died, in whose life we now live. This gives us the power to follow our Surety as our Example: Christ being our Head is the bond that makes the believing in the Surety and the following of the Example inseparably one.

These three are one. The three truths may not be separated from each other. And yet, this happens much too often. There are some who wish to follow Christ's Example without faith in His atonement. They seek to find within themselves, the power to live like Him: their efforts are in vain. There are others who firmly believe in the Suretyship but neglect the Example. They believe in redemption through the blood of the cross, but neglect the footsteps of Him who bore it. Faith in the atonement is indeed the foundation of the building, but it is not all. Theirs, too, is a deficient Christianity, with no true view of sanctification, because they do not see how, along with faith in Christ's atonement, following His Example is indispensably necessary.

There are still others who have received these two truths—Christ as Surety and Christ as Example—and yet lack something. They feel constrained to follow Christ as Example in what He did as Surety, but want the power. They do not properly understand how this following His Example can really be attained. What they need is clear insight into what Scripture teaches of Christ as Head. Because the Surety is not someone outside of me, but One in whom I am, and who is in me, I can become like Him. His very life lives in me. He lives Himself in me, whom He bought with His blood.

To follow His footsteps is a duty. Because it is a possibility, it is the natural result of the wonderful union between Head and members. It is only when this is understood correctly that the blessed truth of Christ's Example will take its right place. If Jesus Himself, through His life union, will work the life likeness in me, then my duty becomes plain and glorious. I have, on the one side, to gaze on His Example so as to know and follow it. On the other, I have to abide in Him, and open my heart to the blessed workings of His life in me. As surely as He conquered sin and its curse *for me,* will He conquer it in its power *in me.* What He began by His death for me, He will perfect by His life in me. Because my Surety is also my Head, His Example must and will be the rule of my life.

There is a saying of Augustine that is often quoted: "Lord! give what Thou commandest, and command what Thou wilt." This holds true here. If the Lord, who lives in me, *gives* what He requires of me, then no requirement can be too high. Then, I will have the courage to gaze on His holy Example in all its height and breadth, and to accept it as the law of my conduct. It is no longer merely a command telling what I must be, but a promise of what I will be. There is nothing that weakens the power of Christ's Example so much as the thought that we cannot really walk like Him. Do not listen to such thoughts. The perfect likeness in heaven is begun on earth, can grow with each day, and will become more visible as life goes on. As certain and mighty as the work of surety which Christ, your Head, completed once and for all, is the renewal after His own image, which He is still working out. Let this double blessing make the cross doubly precious: Our Head suffered as a Surety, that in union with us He might bear sin for us. Our Head suffered as an Example, that He might show us the path on which, in union with Himself, He would lead us to victory and to glory. The suffering Christ is our Head, our Surety, and our Example.

And so, the great lesson I have to learn is the wonderful truth that it is in that mysterious path of suffering—in which He worked out our atonement and redemption that we are to follow His footsteps. The full experience of that redemption depends on the personal fellowship in that suffering. "Christ suffered *for us,* leaving us an Example." May the Holy Spirit reveal to me what this means.

Precious Savior! how can I thank You for the work that You have done as Surety? Standing in the place of me, a guilty sinner, You have borne my sins in Your body on the cross. That cross was my due. You took it, and were made like me, that thus the cross might be changed into a place of blessing and life.

And now You call me to the place of crucifixion as the place of blessing and life. There, I may be made like You, and may find in You power to suffer and to cease from sin. As my Head, You were my Surety to suffer and die with me; as my Head, You are my Example that I might suffer and die with You.

Precious Savior! I confess that I have too little understood this. Your Suretyship was more to me than Your Example. I rejoiced much that You had borne the cross for me, but too little that I, like You and with You, might also bear the cross. The atonement of the cross was more precious to me than the fellowship of the cross. The hope in Your redemption was more precious than personal fellowship with You.

Forgive me this, dear Lord, and teach me to find my happiness in union with You, my Head, and not more in Your Suretyship than in Your Example. And grant that, in my meditations as to how I am to follow You, my faith may become stronger and brighter: Jesus is my Example because He is my life. I must and can be like Him, because I am one with Him. Grant this, my blessed Lord, for Your love's sake. Amen.

Chapter 5

LIKE CHRIST...
In Suffering Wrong

"For this is thankworthy, if a man for conscience toward God endure grief, suffering wrongfully. For what glory is it, if, when ye be buffeted for your faults, ye shall take it patiently? but if, when ye do well, and suffer for it, ye take it patiently, this is acceptable with God"—1 Peter 2:19-20.

Peter uttered those weighty words concerning Christ as our Surety and Example in connection with a very common matter. He is writing to servants who, at that time, were mostly slaves. He teaches them "to be subject with all," not only to the good and gentle, but also to the harsh and cruel. For, so he writes, if any one do wrong and be punished for it, to bear it patiently is no special grace. But, if one does well, suffers it, and takes it patiently, this is acceptable with God; such bearing of wrong is Christlike. In bearing our sins as Surety, Christ suffered wrong from man. Following His example, we must be ready to suffer wrongfully, too.

There is almost nothing harder to bear than injustice from our fellow-men. Besides the sense of pain, there is the feeling of humiliation and injustice, and the consciousness of our rights being violated. In what our fellow-men do to us, it is not easy to at once recognize the will of God, who thus allows us to be tried, to see if we have truly taken Christ as our Example. Let us study that Example. From Him, we may learn what it was that gave Him the power to bear injuries patiently.

Christ believed in suffering as the will of God. He found in Scripture that the servant of God should suffer. He made Himself familiar with the thought, so that when suffering came, it did not take Him by surprise. He expected it. He knew that thus He must be perfected. And so, His first thought was not how to be delivered from it, but how to glorify God in it. This enabled Him to bear the greatest injustice quietly. He saw God's hand in it.

Christian! do you want to have strength to suffer wrong in the spirit in which Christ did? Accustom yourself, in everything that happens, to recognize the hand and will of God. This lesson is of more importance than you think. Whether there is some great wrong done you, or some little offense that you meet in daily life, before you fix your thoughts on the person who did it, be still and remember, *God allows me to come into this trouble to see if I will glorify Him in it.* This trial, be it the greatest or least, is allowed by God, and is His will concerning me. Let me first recognize and submit to *God's will* in it. Then, in the rest of soul which this gives, I will receive wisdom to know how to behave in it. With my eye turned from man to God, suffering wrong is not as hard as it seems.

Christ also believed that God would care for His rights and honor. There is an innate sense of right within us that comes from God. But he who lives in the visible wants his honor to at once be vindicated here below. He who lives in the eternal is satisfied to leave the vindication of his rights and honor in God's hands. He knows that they are safe with Him. It was thus with the Lord Jesus. Peter writes, "He committed Himself to Him that judgeth righteously" (1 Peter 2:23). It was a settled thing between the Father and the Son—the Son was not to care for His own honor, but only for the Father's. The Father would care for the Son's honor. Let the Christian follow Christ's example in this, and it will give him such rest and peace. Give your right and your honor into God's keeping. Meet every offense that man commits against you with the firm trust that God will watch over and care for you. Commit it to Him who judges righteously.

Further, *Christ believed in the power of suffering love.* We all admit that there is no power like that of love. Through it, Christ overcomes the enmity of the world. Every other victory only gives a forced submission. Love alone gives the true victory over an enemy, by converting him into a friend. We all acknowledge the truth of this as a principle, but we shrink from the application. Christ believed it, and acted accordingly. He also said, I will have my revenge; but His revenge was that of love, bringing enemies as friends to His feet. He believed that by silence and submission, and by suffering and bearing wrong, He would win the cause because love would have its triumph.

And this is what He desires of us, too. In our sinful nature, there is more faith in might and right than in the heavenly power of love. But, he who wants to be like Christ must follow Him in this also, that He seeks to conquer evil with good. *The more another does him wrong, the more he feels called to love him.* Even if it is necessary for the offender to be punished by law, he makes sure that there is no personal vendetta involved. As far as he is concerned, he forgives and loves.

Ah, what a difference it would make in Christendom and in our churches if Christ's example were followed! If each one who was reviled, "reviled not again"; if each one who suffered, "threatened not; but committed Himself to Him that judgeth righteously" (1 Peter 2:23). Fellow Christians, this is literally what the Father would have us do. Let us read and read again the words of Peter, until our soul is filled with the thought, "If, when ye do well, and suffer for it, ye take it patiently, *this is acceptable with God.*"

In ordinary Christian life, where we mostly seek to fulfill our calling as redeemed ones in our own strength, such a conformity to the Lord's image is an impossibility. But, in a life of full surrender, where we have given all into His hands in the faith that He will work all in us, there the glorious expectation that the imitation of Christ is indeed within our reach is awakened. For the command to suffer like Christ has come in connection with the teaching, "Christ also suffered for us...that we, being dead to sins, should live unto righteousness" (1 Peter 2:24).

Beloved fellow Christian! would you not love to be like Jesus, and in bearing injuries act as He Himself would have acted in your place? Is it not a glorious prospect in everything, even in this, too, to be conformed to Him? For our strength it is too high. In His strength it is possible. Only surrender yourself to Him daily to be just what He would have you be. Believe that He lives in heaven to be the life and the strength of each one who seeks to walk in His footsteps. Yield yourself to be one with the suffering, crucified Christ, so that you may understand what it is to be dead to sins, and to live unto righteousness. And you will joyfully experience the wonderful power there is in Jesus' death, not only to atone for sin, but to break its power; and in His resurrection, to make you live unto righteousness. You will find it *equally as blessed to fully follow the footsteps of the suffering Savior*, as it has been to trust fully and only in that suffering for atonement and redemption. Christ will be as precious as your Example as He has been as your Surety. Because He took your sufferings upon Himself, you will lovingly take His sufferings upon yourself. And, bearing wrong will become a glorious part of the fellowship with His holy sufferings. It will be a glorious mark of being conformed to His most holy likeness, and a most blessed fruit of the true life of faith.

O Lord my God, I have heard Your precious word: If any man endure grief, suffering wrongfully, and take it patiently, this is acceptable with God. This is indeed a sacrifice that is well-pleasing to You, a work that Your own grace alone has worked, a fruit of the suffering of Your beloved Son, of the example He left, and the power He gives in virtue of His having destroyed the power of sin. O my Father, teach me and all Your children to aim at nothing less than complete conformity to Your dear Son in this trait of His blessed image. Lord my God, I would now, once and for all, give up the keeping of my honor and my rights into Your hands, never again to take charge of them myself. You will care for them most perfectly. May my only care be the honor and the rights of my Lord!

I especially beseech You to fill me with faith in the conquering power of suffering love. Let me fully comprehend how the suffering Lamb of God teaches us that patience and silence and suffering avail more with God, and therefore with man, too, than might or right. O my Father, I must, I would, walk in the footsteps of my Lord Jesus. Let Your Holy Spirit and the light of Your love and presence be my guide and strength. Amen.

Chapter 6

LIKE CHRIST...
Crucified With Him

"I am crucified with Christ: nevertheless I live; yet not I, but Christ liveth in me.... God forbid that I should glory, save in the cross of our Lord Jesus Christ, by whom the world is crucified unto me, and I unto the world"—Galatians 2:20; 6:14.

Taking up the cross was always spoken of by Christ as the test of discipleship. On three different occasions (Matthew 10:38; 16:24; Luke 14:27), we find the words repeated, "If any man will come after Me, let him take up his cross and follow Me." While the Lord was still on His way to the cross, this expression—taking up the cross—was the most appropriate to indicate that conformity to Him to which the disciple is called. But now that He has been crucified, the Holy Spirit gives another expression in which our entire conformity to Christ is still more powerfully set forth—the believing disciple is himself crucified with Christ. The cross is the chief mark of the Christian as it was of Christ. The crucified Christ and the crucified Christian belong to each other. One of the chief elements of likeness to Christ consists of being crucified with Him. Whoever wishes to be like Him must seek to understand the secret of fellowship with His cross.

At first sight, the Christian who seeks conformity to Jesus is afraid of this truth. He shrinks from the painful suffering and death with which the thought of the cross is connected. As His spiritual discernment becomes clearer, however, this word becomes his entire hope and joy. He glories in the cross because it makes him a partner in a death and victory that has already been accomplished, and in which the deliverance from the powers of the flesh and of the world has been secured to him. To understand this, we must carefully notice the language of Scripture.

"I am crucified with Christ," Paul says, "nevertheless I live; yet not I, but Christ liveth in me" (Galatians 2:20). Through faith in Christ we become partakers of Christ's life. That life is a life that has passed through the death of the cross, and *in which the power of that death is always working.* When I receive that life, I receive, at the same moment, the full power of the death on the cross working in me in its never-ceasing energy. "I am crucified with Christ: nevertheless I live; yet not I, but Christ liveth in me." The life I now live is not my own life. The life of the Crucified One is the life of the cross. Being crucified is a thing past and done. "Knowing this, that our old man is crucified with Him"; "They that are Christ's *have* crucified the flesh"; "I glory in the cross of our

Lord Jesus Christ, by whom the world is crucified unto me, and I unto the world" (Romans 6:6; Galatians 5:24; 6:14). These texts all speak of something that has been done in Christ, and into which I am admitted by faith.

It is of great consequence to understand this, and to give bold utterance to the truth: I have been crucified with Christ; I have crucified the flesh. I thus learn how perfectly I share in the finished work of Christ. If I am crucified and dead with Him, then I am a partner in His life and victory. I learn to understand the position I must take to allow the power of that cross and that death to manifest itself in mortifying or making dead the old man and the flesh, in destroying the body of sin (see Romans 6:6).

For there is still a great work for me to do. But, that work is not to crucify myself: I have been crucified; the old man was crucified, so Scripture says. But, what I have to do is to always regard and treat it as crucified, and not to suffer it to come down from the cross. I must maintain my crucifixion position. I must keep the flesh in the place of crucifixion. To realize the force of this I must notice an important distinction. I have been crucified and am dead: the old Adam was crucified, but is not yet dead.

When I gave myself to my crucified Savior, sin and flesh and all, He took me wholly. I with my evil nature was taken up with Him in His crucifixion. But, here a separation took place. In fellowship with Him, I was freed from the life of the flesh. I myself died with Him. In the innermost center of my being, I received new life: Christ lives in *me.* But the flesh, in which I yet am—the old man that was crucified with Him—remained condemned to an accursed death, but is not yet dead. And now it is my calling, in fellowship with and in the strength of my Lord, to see that the old nature be kept nailed to the cross, until the time comes when it is entirely destroyed. All its desires and affections cry out, "Come down from the cross. Save yourself and us." It is my duty to glory in the cross, with my whole heart to maintain the dominion of the cross, to set my seal to the sentence that has been pronounced, to make every uprising of sin dead, already crucified, and not to allow it to have dominion.

This is what Scripture means when it says, "If ye through the spirit do mortify the deeds of the body, ye shall live" (Romans 8:13). "Mortify therefore your members which are upon the earth" (Colossians 3:5). Thus, I continually and voluntarily acknowledge that in my flesh dwells no good thing. My Lord is Christ the Crucified One, and I have been crucified and *am dead* in Him. The flesh has been crucified and, though not yet dead, has been forever given over to the death of the cross. And so, I live like Christ, in very deed crucified with Him.

In order to fully enter into the meaning and the power of this fellowship of the crucifixion of our Lord, two things especially are necessary to those who are Christ's followers. The first is the clear consciousness of their fellowship with the Crucified

One through faith. At conversion, they became partakers of it without fully understanding it. Many remain in ignorance all their life long because of a lack of spiritual knowledge. Brother and sister, pray that the Holy Spirit may reveal to you your union to the Crucified One. "I am crucified with Christ." "I glory in the cross of our Lord Jesus Christ, by whom the world is crucified unto me" (Galatians 6:14). Take such words of Holy Scripture, and, by prayer and meditation, make them your own with a heart that expects and asks the Holy Spirit to make them living and effectual within you. Look upon yourself in the light of what you really are, "crucified with Christ."

Then you will find the grace for the second thing you need to enable you to live as a crucified one, in whom Christ lives. You will always be able to look upon and to treat the flesh and the world as nailed to the cross. The old nature continually seeks to assert itself, and to make you feel as if it is expecting too much to always live this crucifixion life. Your only safety is in fellowship with Christ. "Through Him and His cross," says Paul, "I am crucified to the world." In Him, the crucifixion is an accomplished reality. In Him, you have died, but also have been made alive: Christ lives in you. The deeper this fellowship of His cross is in you, the better. It brings you into deeper communion with His life and His love. To be crucified with Christ means freed from the power of sin—a redeemed one, a conqueror. Remember that the Holy Spirit has been specially provided to glorify Christ in you, to reveal within you, and make your very own, all that is in Christ for you.

Do not be satisfied, as so many others, to only know the cross in its power to atone. The glory of the cross is, not only to Jesus, but to us, too, the path to life. But, each moment it can become to us the power that destroys sin and death, and keeps us in the power of the eternal life. Learn from your Savior the holy art of using it for this. Faith in the power of the cross and its victory will day by day make dead the deeds of the body, the lusts of the flesh. This faith will teach you to regard the cross, with its continual death to self, as all your glory. Regard the cross, not as one who is still on the way to crucifixion—with the prospects of a painful death—but as one to whom the crucifixion is past, who already lives in Christ, and now only bears the cross as the blessed instrument through which the body or sin is done away (see Romans 6:6). The banner under which complete victory over sin and the world is to be won is the cross.

Above all, remember what still remains the chief thing. It is Jesus, the living, loving Savior, who Himself enables you to be like Him in all things. His sweet fellowship, His tender love, and His heavenly power make it a blessedness and joy to be like Him, the Crucified One. They make the crucifixion life a life of resurrection-joy and power. In Him, the two are inseparably connected. In Him, you have the strength to always be singing the triumphant song:

God forbid that I should glory, save in the cross of our Lord Jesus Christ, through which the world has been crucified unto me, and I unto the world.

Precious Savior, I humbly ask You to show me the hidden glory of the fellowship of Your cross. The cross was my place, the place of death and curse. You became like us, and have been crucified with us. And now the cross is Your place, the place of blessing and life. You call me to become like You, and as one who is crucified with You, to experience how entirely the cross has made me free from sin.

Lord, give me to know its full power. It is long since I knew the power of the cross to redeem from the curse. But how long I strove in vain as a redeemed one to overcome the power of sin, and to obey the Father as You have done! I could not break the power of sin. But now I see, this comes only when Your disciple yields himself entirely to be led by the Holy Spirit into the fellowship of Your cross. There You let him see how the cross *has broken forever* the power of sin, and has made him free. There You, the Crucified One, live in him and impart to him Your own Spirit of wholehearted self-sacrifice, in casting out and conquering sin. Oh, my Lord, teach me to understand this better. In this faith I say, "I have been crucified with Christ." Oh, You who loved me to the death, not Your cross, but Yourself the Crucified One, You are He whom I seek and in whom I hope. Take me, Crucified One, hold me fast, and teach me from moment to moment to look upon all that is of self as condemned, and only worthy to be crucified. Take me, hold me, and teach me, from moment to moment, that in You I have all I need for a life of holiness and blessing. Amen.

Chapter 7

LIKE CHRIST...
In His Self-Denial

"We then that are strong ought to bear the infirmities of the weak, and not to please ourselves. Let every one of us please his neighbor for his good to edification. For even Christ pleased not himself; but as it is written, The reproaches of them that reproached thee fell on me.... Wherefore receive ye one another, as Christ also received us to the glory of God"—Romans 15:1-3,7.

"If any man will come after me, let him deny himself, and take up his cross, and follow me"—Matthew 16:24.

Even Christ did not please Himself. He bore the reproaches, with which men reproached and dishonored God, so patiently so that He could glorify God and save man. Christ pleased not Himself: referring to both God and man, this word is the key of His life. In this, too, His life is our rule and example; we who are strong ought not to please ourselves.

To deny self is the opposite of pleasing self. When Peter denied Christ, he said: I do not know the man.

I have nothing to do with Him and His interests. I do not wish to be counted His friend. In the same way, the true Christian denies himself, the old man: I do not know this old man. I will have nothing to do with him and his interests. And when shame and dishonor come upon him, or when anything happens that is not pleasant to the old nature, he simply says: Do as you like with the old Adam, I will take no notice of it. Through the cross of Christ I am crucified to the world, the flesh, and self. To the friendship and interest of this old man I am a stranger. I deny him to be my friend; I deny his every claim and wish. I know him not.

The Christian who only thinks of his salvation from curse and condemnation cannot understand this. He finds it impossible to deny self. Although he may sometimes try to do so, his life mainly consists of pleasing himself. The Christian who has taken Christ as his example cannot be content with this. He has surrendered himself to seek the most complete fellowship with the cross of Christ. The Holy Spirit has taught him to say, I have been crucified with Christ, and so am dead to sin and self. In fellowship with Christ, he sees the old man crucified, a condemned criminal. He is ashamed to know him as a friend. It is his fixed purpose, and he has also received the power for it—no longer is he to please his old nature, but to deny it. *Because the crucified Christ is his life, self-denial is the law of his life.*

This self-denial extends itself over the whole domain of life. It was so with the Lord Jesus, and is to be so with everyone who longs to follow Him perfectly. This self-denial is not as concerned with what is sinful, unlawful, and contrary to the laws of God, as with what is lawful, or apparently indifferent. To the self-denying spirit, the will and glory of God, and the salvation of man are always to be more important than our own interests or pleasure.

Before we can know how to please our neighbor, self-denial must first exercise itself in our own personal life. It must rule the body. The holy fasting of Him who said, "Man shall not live by bread alone, but by every word that proceedeth out of the mouth of God" (Matthew 4:4), who would not eat until His Father gave Him food, and His Father's work was done, teaches the believer a holy temperance in eating and drinking. The holy poverty of Him who had nowhere to lay His head, teaches the believer to regulate the possession, use, and enjoyment of earthly things, so that he may always possess as not possessing. After the example of the holy suffering of Him who bore all our sins in His own body on the tree, the believer learns to bear all suffering patiently. Even in the body as the temple of the Holy Spirit, he desires to bear the dying of the Lord Jesus. With Paul, he denies the body and brings it into subjection; all its desires and appetites he would have ruled by the self-denial of Jesus. He does not please himself.

This self-denial keeps watch over the spirit, too. The believer brings his own wisdom and judgment into subjection to God's Word. He gives up his own thoughts to the teaching of the Word and the Spirit. Toward man, he manifests the same self-denial of his own wisdom in a readiness to hear and to learn. In the meekness and humility with which, even when he knows he is right, he gives his opinion, desiring to always find and acknowledge what is good in others.

And then, self-denial has special reference to the heart. All the affections and desires are placed under it. The will, and the kingly power of the soul are especially under its control. As little as self-pleasing could be a part of Christ's life, may Christ's follower allow it to be a part of his life, or allow it to influence his conduct. "We ought not to please ourselves. For even Christ pleased not Himself." Self-denial is the law of his life.

Nor does the believer find self-denial hard once he has truly surrendered himself to it. To one who, with a divided heart, seeks to force himself to a life of self-denial, it is indeed hard. But, to one who has yielded himself to it unreservedly—because he has with his whole heart accepted the cross to destroy the power of sin and self—the blessing it brings more than compensates for apparent sacrifice or loss. He hardly thinks any longer about self-denial, because there is such blessedness in becoming conformed to the image of Jesus.

Self-denial is not valuable with God, as some think, because of the measure of pain it causes. No, for this pain is very much caused by the remaining reluctance to practice it. But, it has its highest worth in that meek or even joyful acquiescence which counts nothing a sacrifice for Jesus' sake, and feels surprised when others speak of self-denial.

There have been ages when men thought they must fly to the wilderness or become hermits to deny themselves. The Lord Jesus has shown us that the best place to practice self-denial is in our ordinary fellowship with men. So Paul also says here, *"We ought not to please ourselves,* let every one please his *neighbor unto edification. For even Christ pleased not Himself....* Wherefore receive ye one another, *as Christ* also received us." Nothing less than the self-denial of our Lord, who pleased not Himself, is our law. What He was we must be. What He did we must do.

What a glorious life there will be in the Church of Christ when this law prevails! Each one considers it the object of existence to make others happy. Each one denies himself, seeks not his own, and esteems others better than himself. All thought of taking offense, of wounded pride, of being slighted or passed by, would pass away. As a follower of Christ, each would seek to bear the weak and to please his neighbor. The true self-denial would be seen in this—that no one would think of himself, but live in and for others.

"If any man will *come after* Me, let him deny himself, take up his cross, and *follow Me."* This word not only gives us the will, but also the power for self-denial. He who does not simply wish to reach heaven through Christ, but comes after Him for His own sake, will *follow* Him. And in his heart, Jesus speedily takes the place that self had. *Jesus only* becomes the center and object of such a life. The undivided surrender to follow Him is crowned with this wonderful blessing—Christ by His Spirit Himself becomes his life. Christ's spirit of self-denying love is poured out upon him, and to deny self is the greatest joy of his heart and the means of the deepest communion with God. Self-denial is no longer a work he simply does in order to attain perfection for himself. Nor is it merely a negative victory, of which the main feature is keeping self in check. Christ has taken the place of self, and His love and gentleness and kindness flow out to others, now that self is parted with. No command becomes more blessed or more natural than this: *"We ought not to please ourselves, for even Christ pleased not Himself."* "If any man come after Me, let him deny himself, and *follow Me."*

Beloved Lord, I thank You for this new call to follow You and not to please myself, even as You did not please Yourself. I thank You that I no longer have to hear it with fear as I once did. Your commandments are no longer grievous to me. Your yoke is easy, and Your burden light. What I see in Your life on earth as my example is the certain pledge of what I receive from Your life in heaven. I did not always understand it so. Long after I had known You, I dared not think of self-denial. But, for him who has learned what it is to take up the cross, to be crucified with You, and to see the old man nailed to the cross, it is no longer terrible to deny it. Oh, my Lord! who would not be ashamed to be the friend of a crucified and accursed criminal?

Since I have learned that You are my life, and that You wholly take charge of the life that is wholly intrusted to You, to work both to will and to do, I do not fear that you will not give me the love and wisdom in the path of self-denial to joyfully follow Your footsteps. Blessed Lord, Your disciples are not worthy of this grace. But, since You have chosen us to it, we will gladly seek not to please ourselves but everyone his neighbor, as You have taught us. And may the Holy Spirit work it in us mightily. Amen.

Chapter 8

LIKE CHRIST . . .
In His Self-Sacrifice

"Walk in love, as Christ also hath loved us, and hath given himself for us an offering and a sacrifice to God for a sweet-smelling savour"—Ephesians 5:2.

"Hereby perceive we the love of God, because he laid down his life for us: and we ought to lay down our lives for the brethren"—1 John 3:16.

What is the connection between self-sacrifice and self-denial? The former is the root from which the latter springs. In self-denial, self-sacrifice is tested. It is thus strengthened and prepared each time to renew its entire surrender. Thus it was with the Lord Jesus. His incarnation was a self-sacrifice. His life of self-denial was the proof of it. Through this, He was prepared for the great act of self-sacrifice in His death on the cross. Thus it is with the Christian. His conversion is, to a certain extent, the sacrifice of self, though a very partial one due to ignorance and weakness. From that first act of self-surrender arises the obligation to the exercise of daily self-denial.

The Christian's efforts to do so show him his weakness, and prepare him for that new and more entire self-sacrifice in which he first finds strength for more continuous self-denial.

Self-sacrifice is of the very essence of true love. The very nature and blessedness of love consists in forgetting self, and seeking happiness in the loved one. Where there is a want or need in the beloved, love is impelled, by its very nature, to offer up its own happiness for that of the other, to unite itself to the beloved one, and at any sacrifice to make him the sharer of its own blessedness.

Who can say whether or not this is one of the secrets which eternity will reveal: that sin was permitted because otherwise God's love could never have been so fully revealed? The highest glory of God's love was manifested in the self-sacrifice of Christ. It is the highest glory of the Christian to be like his Lord in this. Without entire self-sacrifice, the new command, the command of love, cannot be fulfilled. Without entire self-sacrifice, we cannot love as Jesus loved. "Be ye imitators of God," says the apostle, "and walk in love, even as Christ hath loved us, and given Himself a sacrifice for us." Let all your walk and conversation be, according to Christ's example, in love. It was this love that made His sacrifice acceptable in God's sight, a sweet-smelling savor. As His love exhibited itself in self-sacrifice, let your love prove itself to be conformable to His in the daily self-sacrifice for the welfare of others. Thus will it also be acceptable in the sight of

God. "We ought to lay down our lives for the brethren."

Even in the daily affairs of home life, in the discourse between husband and wife, and in the relationship of master and servant, Christ's self-sacrifice must be the rule of our walk. "Likewise, ye husbands, love your wives, even as also Christ loved the Church, and *gave Himself for it"* (Ephesians 5:25).

And especially notice the words, "Hath given Himself *for us* an offering *to God."* We see that self-sacrifice has two sides. Christ's self-sacrifice had a Godward as well as a manward aspect. It was *for us,* but it was *to God* that He offered Himself as a sacrifice. In all our self-sacrifice, there must be these two sides in union, though, at times, the one may be more prominent than the other.

It is only when we sacrifice ourselves *to God* that we will find the power for an entire self-sacrifice. The Holy Spirit reveals to the believer God's claim on us, how we are not our own, but His. The realization of how absolutely we are God's property, bought and paid for with blood, of how we are loved with such a wonderful love, and of what blessedness there is in the full surrender to Him, leads the believer to yield himself a whole burnt offering. He lays himself on the altar of consecration, and finds it his highest joy to be a sweet-smelling savor *to his God*—God-devoted and God-accepted. And then, it becomes his first and most earnest desire to know how God wants him to show this entire self-sacrifice in life and walk.

God points him to Christ's example. He was a sweet-smelling savor to God when He gave Himself a sacrifice *for us.* For every Christian who gives himself entirely to His service, God bestows the same honor as He did for His Son—He uses him as an instrument of blessing to others. Therefore, John says, "He that loveth not his brother whom he hath seen, how can he love God whom he hath not seen?" (1 John 4:20). The self-sacrifice in which you have devoted yourself to God's service binds you also to serve your fellow-men. The same act which makes us entirely God's makes you entirely theirs.

It is this surrender to God that gives the power for self-sacrifice toward others, and even makes it a joy. When faith has first appropriated the promise, "Inasmuch as ye have done it to unto one of the least of these My brethren, ye have done it unto Me" (Matthew 25:40), I understand the glorious harmony between sacrifice *to God* and sacrifice *for men.* My fellowship with my fellow-men, instead of being, as many complain, a hindrance to unbroken communion with God, becomes an opportunity of offering myself unceasingly to Him.

Blessed calling! to walk in love even as Christ loved us, and gave Himself for us a sacrifice and sweet-smelling savor to God. Only thus can the Church fulfill its destiny, prove to the world that she is set apart to continue Christ's work of self-sacrificing love, and fill up that which remains behind of the afflictions of Christ.

But does God really expect us to deny ourselves so

entirely for others? Is it not asking too much? Can any one really sacrifice himself so entirely? Christian! God does expect it. Nothing less than this is the conformity to the image of His Son, to which He predestinated you from eternity. This is the path by which Jesus entered into His glory and blessedness, and by no other way can the disciple enter into the joy of His Lord. *It is in very deed our calling to become exactly like Jesus in His love and Self-sacrifice.* "Walk in love, as Christ loved."

It is a great thing when a believer sees and acknowledges this. That God's people and even God's servants understand it so little is one great cause of the weakness of the Church. In this matter, the Church indeed needs a second reformation. In the great Reformation three centuries ago, the power of Christ's atoning death and righteousness were brought to light—to the great comfort and joy of anxious souls. But, we need a second reformation to lift on high the banner of Christ's example as our law, and to restore the truth of the power of Christ's resurrection as it makes us partakers of the life and the likeness of our Lord. Christians must not only believe in the full union with their Surety for their reconciliation, but with their Head as their example and their life. They must really represent Christ on earth, and *let men see in the members* how the Head lived when He was in the flesh. Let us earnestly pray that God's children everywhere may be taught to see their holy calling.

And all you who already long for it, oh, fear not to

yield yourselves to God in the great act of a Christ-like self-sacrifice! In conversion, you gave yourself to God. In many an act of self-surrender since then you have again given yourselves to Him. But, experience has taught you how much is still wanting. Perhaps you never knew how entire the self-sacrifice must and could be. Come now and see in Christ your example, and in His sacrifice of Himself on the cross, *what your Father expects of you.* Come now and see in Christ—for He is your head and life—*what He will enable you to be and do.* Believe in Him, that what He accomplished on earth in His life and death as your example, He will now accomplish in you from heaven. Offer yourself to the Father in Christ, with the desire to be, as entirely and completely as He, an offering and a sacrifice unto God, *given up to God for men.*

Expect Christ to work this in you and to maintain it. Let your relationship to God be clear and distinct—you, like Christ, wholly given up to Him. Then, it will no longer be impossible to walk in love as Christ loved us. Then, all your fellowship with the brethren and with the world will be the most glorious opportunity of proving before God how completely you have given yourself to *Him,* an offering and a sacrifice for a sweet-smelling savor.

O my God, who am I that You should have chosen me to be conformed to the image of Your Son in His self-sacrificing love? In this is His divine perfection and glory, that He loved not His own life, but freely offered it for us to You in death. And in this I may be like Him. In a walk in love I may prove that I, too, have offered myself wholly to God.

O my Father, Your purpose is mine. At this solemn moment I reaffirm my consecration to You. Not in my own strength, but in the strength of Him who gave Himself for me. Because Christ, my example, is also my life, I venture to say it: Father, in Christ, like Christ, I yield myself a sacrifice to You for men.

Father, teach me how You would use me to manifest Your love to the world. You will do it by filling me full of Your love. Father, do it, that I may walk in love, *even as* Christ loved us. May I live every day as one who has the power of the Holy Spirit to enable me to love everyone I come into contact with. Under every possible circumstance, let me love with a love which is not of me, but of Yourself. Amen.

Chapter 9

LIKE CHRIST... *Not Of The World*

"These are in the world.... The world hath hated them, because they are not of the world, even as I am not of the world.... They are not of the world, even as I am not of the world"—John 17:11,14,16.

"As he is, so are we in this world"—1 John 4:17.

If Jesus was not *of* the world, why was He *in* the world? If there was no sympathy between Him and the world, why was it that He lived in it, and did not remain in that high, holy, and blessed world to which He belonged? The answer is—the Father had sent Him into the world. In these two expressions, "In the world," and "Not of the world," we find the whole secret of His work as Savior, of His glory as the God-man.

In the world, in human nature, because God wanted to show that this nature belonged to Him, and not to the god of this world, that this nature was most fit to receive the divine life, and in this divine life to reach its highest glory.

In the world, in fellowship with men, to enter into

a loving relationship with them, to be seen and known of them, and thus to win them back to the Father.

In the world, in the struggle with the powers which rule the world, to learn obedience, and so to perfect and sanctify human nature.

Not of the world, but of heaven, to manifest and bring near the life that is in God, which man had lost, that men might see and long for it.

Not of the world, witnessing against its sin and departure from God, its inability to know and please God.

Not of the world, founding a Kingdom entirely heavenly in origin and nature, entirely independent of all that the world holds desirable or necessary, and with principles and laws the very opposite of those which rule in the world.

Not of the world, in order to redeem all who belong to Him, and bring them into that new and heavenly Kingdom which He had revealed.

In the world; Not of the world. In these two expressions we have revealed to us the great mystery of the person and work of the Savior. "Not *of* the world," in the power of His divine holiness judging and overcoming it; still *in* the world, and through His humanity and love seeking and saving all that can be saved. The most entire separation from the world, with the closest fellowship with those in the world—these two extremes meet in Jesus. In His own person, He has reconciled them. And, it is the calling of the Christian in his life to prove that these two dispositions, however much they may seem at variance, can in our life, too, be united in perfect harmony. In each believer, there must be a heavenly life shining out through earthly forms.

To take one of these two truths and exclusively cultivate it is not so difficult. So you have those who have taken "Not of the world" as their motto. From the earliest ages, when people thought they must fly to cloisters and deserts to serve God, to our own days, when some seek to show the earnestness of their piety by severity in judging all that is in the world, there have been those who counted this the only true Christianity. There was separation from sin, but then there was also no fellowship with sinners. The sinner could not feel that he was surrounded with the atmosphere of a tender, heavenly love. It was a one-sided, and therefore a defective, faith.

Then, there are those who, on the other hand, stress "In the world," and very specially appeal to the words of the apostle, "For then must ye needs go out of the world" (1 Corinthians 5:10). They think that by showing that Christianity does not make us unfriendly or unfit to enjoy all that there is to enjoy, they will induce the world to serve God. It has often happened that they have indeed succeeded in making the world very religious, but at too high a price—Christianity became very worldly.

The true follower of Jesus must combine both. If he does not clearly show that he is not of the world, and prove the greater blessedness of a heavenly life, how will he convince the world of sin, prove to her that there is a higher life, or teach her to desire what she does not yet possess? Earnestness, holiness, and separation from the spirit of the world must characterize him. His heavenly spirit must manifest that he belongs to a Kingdom not of this world. An unworldly, other-worldly, heavenly spirit must breath in him. .

And still, he must live as one who is "in the world." He was expressly placed here by God, among those who are of the world, to win their hearts, to acquire influence over them, and to communicate to them of the Spirit which is in him. The great study of his life must be how he can fulfill this his mission. He will not succeed—as the wisdom of the world would teach—by yielding, complying, and softening down the solemn realities of Christianity. No, he will succeed only by walking in the footsteps of Him who alone can teach how to be in the world and yet not of it. Only by a life of serving and suffering love, in which the Christian distinctly confesses that the glory of God is the aim of his existence, and in which, full of the Holy Spirit, he brings men into direct contact with the warmth and love of the heavenly life, can he be a blessing to the world.

Oh, who will teach us the heavenly secret of how to unite being *in* the world but not *of* the world in our daily lives? He who has said, "They are not of the world, even as I am not of the world," can do it. That "*even as*" has a deeper meaning and power than we know. If we allow the Holy Spirit to unfold that word to us, we will understand what it is to be in the world as He was in the world. That "*even as*" has its root and strength in a life union. In it, we will discover the divine secret, that *the more entirely one is not of the world, the more fit he is to be in the world.* The freer the Church is of the spirit and principles of the world, the more influence she will exert in it.

The life of the world is self-pleasing and self-exalting. The life of heaven is holy, self-denying love. The weakness of the life of many Christians who seek to separate themselves from the world is that they have too much of the spirit of the world. They seek their own happiness and perfection more than they seek anything else. Jesus Christ was not of the world, and had nothing of its spirit. This is why He could love sinners, could win them, and save them.

The believer is as little of the world as Christ. The Lord says: "Not of the world, even as I am not of the world." In his new nature, he is born from heaven, has the life and love of heaven in him. His supernatural, heavenly life gives him the ability to be in the world without being of it. The disciple who fully believes in the Christlikeness of his inner life will experience the truth of it. He cultivates and gives utterance to the assurance: "Even as Christ, so am I not of the world, because I am in Christ." He understands that only in close union with Christ can his separation from the world be maintained. In as far as Christ lives in him can he lead a heavenly life. He sees that the only way to answer to his calling is, on the one hand, as crucified to the world to withdraw himself from its power; and, on the other, as living in Christ to go into it and bless it. He lives in heaven and walks on earth.

Christians! see here the true imitation of Jesus Christ. "Wherefore come out from among them, and be ye separate, saith the Lord" (2 Corinthians 6:17). Then the promise is fulfilled, "I will dwell in them and walk in them" (2 Corinthians 6:16). Then Christ sends you, as the Father sent Him, to be in the world as the place ordained of your Father to glorify Him, and to make known His love. A truly unworldly, heavenly spirit manifests itself not so much in the desire to leave earth for heaven, as in the willingness to live the life of heaven here on earth.

"Not of the world" is not only separation from and testimony against the world, but it is the living manifestation of the spirit, the love, and the power of the other world—of the heaven to which we belong, in its divine work of making this world partaker of its blessedness.

O great High Priest! who in Your high-priestly power did pray for us to the Father, as those who, no more than Yourself, belong to the world, and still must remain in it, let Your all-prevailing intercession now be effectual in our behalf.

The world still has entrance to our hearts, its selfish spirit is still too much within us. Through unbelief, the new nature has not always had full power. Lord, we beseech You, as fruit of Your all-powerful intercession, let that word be fully realized in us: "Not of the world, even as I am not of the world." Our only power against the world is in our likeness to You.

Lord, we can only be like You when we are one with You. We can only walk like You when we abide in You. Blessed Lord, we surrender ourselves to abide in You alone. A life entirely given to you is one which You take entire possession of. Let the Holy Spirit, who dwells in us, unite us so closely with You that we may always live as *not of the world.* And let Your Spirit so make known to us Your work in the world, that it may be our joy in deep humility and fervent love to exhibit to all what a blessed life there is in the world for those who are not of the world. May the proof that we are not of the world be the tenderness and fervency with which, like You, we sacrifice ourselves for those who are in the world. Amen.

Chapter 10

LIKE CHRIST...
In His Heavenly Mission

"As thou hast sent me into the world, even so have I also sent them into the world"—John 17:18.

"As my Father hath sent me, even so send I you"—John 20:21.

The Lord Jesus lived here on earth under a deep consciousness of having a mission from His Father to fulfill. He continually used the expression, "The Father hath sent Me." He knew what the mission was. He knew the Father had chosen Him, and sent Him into the world with the one purpose of fulfilling that mission. He knew the Father would give Him all that He needed for it. Faith in the Father having sent Him was the motive and power for all that He did.

In earthly things, it is a great help if an ambassador clearly knows what his mission is. That way, he has nothing to do but to care for its accomplishment, and to give himself undividedly to do this one thing. For the Christian, it is no less important that he should know that he has a mission, what its nature is, and how he is to accomplish it.

Our heavenly mission is one of the most glorious parts of our conformity to our Lord. He says it plainly in the most solemn moments of His life: "that even as the Father sent Him," so He sends His disciples. He says it to the Father in His high-priestly prayer, as the basis upon which He asks for their keeping and sanctification. He says it to the disciples after His resurrection, as the basis on which they are to receive the Holy Spirit. Nothing will help us to know and fulfill our mission more than to realize how perfectly it corresponds to the mission of Christ, how they are, in fact, identical.

Our mission is like His *in its object.* Why did the Father send His Son? To make known His love and His will in the salvation of sinners. He was to do this not alone by word and precept, but in His own person, disposition, and conduct, He was to exhibit the Father's holy love. He was so to represent the unseen Father in heaven, that men on earth might know what the Father was like.

After the Lord had fulfilled His mission, He ascended into heaven, and became to the world like the Father, the Unseen One. And now He has given His mission to His disciples, after having shown them how to fulfill it. They must so represent Him, the Invisible One, that from seeing them men can judge what He is. Every Christian must so be the image of Jesus—must so exhibit in his person and conduct the same love to sinners, and desire for their salvation, as animated Christ—that from them the world may know what Christ is like. Oh, my soul!

take time to realize these heavenly thoughts: Our mission is like Christ's in its object, the showing forth of the holy love of heaven in earthly form.

Like Christ's *in its origin, too.* It was the Father's love that chose Christ for this work, and counted Him worthy of such honor and trust. We are also chosen by Christ for this work. Every redeemed one knows that it was not he who sought the Lord, but the Lord who sought and chose him. In that seeking and drawing, the Lord had this heavenly mission in view. "Ye have not chosen Me, but I have chosen you, and ordained you, that ye should go and bring forth fruit" (John 15:16).

Believer! whoever you are, and wherever you dwell, the Lord, who knows you and your surroundings, has need of you, and has chosen you to be His representative in the circle in which you move. Fix your heart on this. He has fixed His heart on you and saved you, in order that you should bear and exhibit to those who surround you the very image of His unseen glory. Oh, think of the origin of your heavenly mission in His everlasting love, as His had its origin in the love of the Father. Your mission is, in very truth, just like His.

Like Christ's, too, *in the fitting for it.* Every ambassador expects to be supplied with all that he needs for his embassy. "He that sent Me is with Me: the Father hath not left Me alone" (John 8:29). That word tells us how, when the Father sent the Son, He was always with Him, His strength and comfort. It is even so with the Church of Christ in her mission:

"Go ye therefore, and teach all nations," has the promise: "Lo, I am with you alway" (Matthew 28:19,20). The Christian need never hold back because of unfitness. The Lord does not demand anything which He does not give the power to perform. Every believer may depend on it. As the Father gave His Holy Spirit to the Son to fit Him for all His work, so the Lord Jesus will give His people all the preparation they need. The grace to show forth Christ evermore, to exhibit the lovely light of His example and likeness, and, like Christ Himself, to be a fountain of love and life and blessing to all around is given to everyone who only heartily and believingly takes up his heavenly calling. In this, too—that the sender cares for all that is needful for the sent ones—is our mission like His.

Our mission is like His *in the consecration which it demands.* The Lord Jesus gave Himself entirely and undividedly over to accomplish His work; He lived for it alone. "I must work the works of Him that sent Me, while it is day: the night cometh when no man can work" (John 9:4). The Father's mission was the only reason for His being on earth. For this alone He would live—to reveal to mankind what a glorious, blessed God the Father of heaven was.

As with Jesus, so with us. Christ's mission is *the only reason for our being on earth.* Were it not for that, He would take us away. Most believers do not believe this. To fulfill Christ's mission is with them at best something to be done along with other things, for which it is difficult to find time and strength. And yet, it is so certainly true that to accomplish Christ's mission is the only reason of my being upon earth. Then when I first believe this, and, like my Lord in His mission, consecrate myself undividedly to it, I will indeed live well-pleasing to Him. This heavenly mission is so great and glorious that without an entire consecration to it we cannot accomplish it. Without this, the powers which fit us for it cannot take possession of us. Without this, we have no liberty to expect the Lord's wonderful help and the fulfillment of all His blessed promises. Just as with Jesus, our heavenly mission demands nothing less than entire consecration. Am I prepared for this? Then I indeed have the key through which the holy glories of this word of Jesus will be revealed to my experience: "As the Father sent Me, even so send I you."

O brothers! this heavenly mission is indeed worthy that we devote ourselves entirely to it as the only thing we live for.

O Lord Jesus! You descended from heaven to earth to show us what the life of heaven is. You could do this because You were of heaven. You brought with You the image and Spirit of the heavenly life to earth. Therefore, did You so gloriously exhibit what constitutes the very glory of heaven—the will and love of the unseen Father.

Lord! You are now the Invisible One in heaven, and send us to represent You in Your heavenly glory as Savior. You ask that we so love men that from us they may form some idea of how You love them in heaven.

Blessed Lord! our heart cries out: How can You send us with such a calling? How can You expect it of us who have so little love? How can we, who are of the earth, show what the life of heaven is?

Precious Savior! our souls do bless You that we know You do not demand more than You give. You who are the life of heaven live in Your disciples. Blessed be Your holy name, they have from You the Holy Spirit from heaven as their life breath. He is the heavenly life of the soul. Whoever surrenders himself to the leading of the Spirit can fulfill his mission. In the joy and power of the Holy Spirit we can be Your image-bearers, can show to men in some measure what Your likeness is.

Lord, teach me and all Your people to understand that we are not of the world, as You were not of the world, and therefore are sent of You, even as You were sent of the Father, to prove in our life that we are of that world, full of love, purity, and blessing, like You were. Amen.

Chapter 11

LIKE CHRIST...
As The Elect of God

"Predestinate to be conformed to the image of his Son, that he might be the firstborn among many brethren"—Romans 8:29.

Scripture teaches us about personal election. It does this not only in single passages, but also gives the whole history of its being worked out here in time through the counsels of eternity. We continually see how the whole future of God's Kingdom depends on the faithful filling of His place by some single person. The only security for the carrying out of God's purpose is His foreordaining of the individual. In predestination alone, the history of the world and of God's Kingdom, as of the individual believer, has its sure foundation.

There are Christians who cannot see this. They are so afraid of interfering with human responsibility that they reject the doctrine of divine predestination because it appears to rob man of his liberty of will and action. Scripture does not share this fear. It speaks in one place of man's free will as though there were no election. In another place, it speaks of election as though there were no free will. Thus, it teaches us that we must hold fast both these truths alongside each other, even when we cannot understand them, or make them harmonize. In the light of eternity, the solution of the mystery will be given. He who grasps both in faith will speedily experience how little they are in conflict. He will see that the stronger his faith is in God's everlasting purpose, the more his courage for work will be strengthened. While, on the other hand, the more he works and is blessed, the clearer it will become that all is of God.

For this reason, it is so important for a believer to make his election sure. The Scriptures give the assurance that if we do this, "ye shall never stumble" (2 Peter 1:10). The more I believe that I am elected of God, and see how this election has reference to every part of my calling, the more I will be strengthened in the conviction that God Himself will perfect His work in me. Therefore, it is possible for me to be all that God really expects. With every duty Scripture lays upon me, with every promise for whose fulfillment I long, I will find, in God's purposes, the firm footing upon which my expectations may rest, and the true measure by which they are to be guided. I will understand that my life on earth is to be a copy of the heavenly life plan, which the Father has drawn out, of what I am to be on earth. Christian! make your calling and election sure. Let it become clear to you that you are elected, and to what. "If ye do these things, ye shall never stumble" (2 Peter 1:10). Quiet communion with God on the ground of His unchangeable purpose imparts an immovable firmness to the soul, and keeps it from stumbling.

One of the most blessed expressions in regard to God's purpose concerning us in Christ is this word: "Predestinate to be conformed to the image of His Son." The man Christ Jesus is the elect of God; in Him, election has its beginning and ending. "In Him we are chosen." For the sake of our union with Him and to His glory, our election took place. The believer who merely seeks the certainty of his own salvation in election, or likewise relief from fear and doubt, knows very little of its real glory. The purposes of election embrace all the riches that are prepared for us in Christ, and reach to every moment and every need of our lives. "Chosen in Him...that we should be holy and without blame before Him in love" (Ephesians 1:4). It is only when the connection between election and sanctification is properly understood in the Church that the doctrine of election will bring its full blessing (see 2 Thessalonians 2:13; 1 Peter 1:2). It teaches the believer how it is God who must work all in him, and how he may rely even in the smallest matters upon the unchangeable purpose of God to work out itself in the accomplishment of everything that He expects of His people. In this light, the word "predestinate to be conformed to the image of His Son" gives new strength to everyone who has begun to take *what Christ is* as the rule of *what he himself is to be.*

Christian! if you in very deed want to be *like*

Christ, fix your mind on the thought of how certainly this is God's will concerning you. Remember how the whole of redemption has been planned with the view of your becoming so, and how God's purpose is the guarantee that your desires must be fulfilled. There, where your name is written in the Book of Life, there stands also, "Predestinate to be conformed to the image of His Son." All the powers of the Deity which have already worked together in the accomplishment of the first part of the eternal purpose—the revealing of the Father's perfect likeness in the man Christ Jesus—are equally engaged to accomplish the second part, and work that likeness in each of God's children. In the work of Christ, there is the most perfect provision possible for the carrying out of God's purpose in this. Our union to Christ, held fast in a living faith, will be an all-prevailing power. We can depend on it as something ordained with a divine certainty, and that must come if we yield ourselves to it. Has God not elected us to be conformed to the image of His Son?

It can easily be understood what a powerful influence the living consciousness of this truth will have. It teaches us to give up ourselves to God's eternal will, that it may, with divine power, effect its purpose in us. It shows us how useless and helpless our own efforts are to accomplish this work. All that is *of* God must also be *through* Him. He who is the beginning must also be the middle and the end. In a very wonderful manner, it strengthens our faith with a holy boldness to glory in God alone, and to expect from God Himself the fulfillment of every promise and every command—of every part of the purpose of His blessed will.

And in what does this likeness to Christ consist? In Sonship. It is to the image of *His Son* we are to be conformed. All the different traits of a Christlike life resolve themselves into this one as their beginning and end. We are "predestinate unto the adoption of *children* by Jesus Christ." It was *as the Son* Christ lived and served and pleased the Father. It is only *as a son*, with the spirit of His own *Son* in my heart, that I can live, serve, and please the Father. I must walk each day in the full and clear consciousness: like Christ, I am a son of the Most High God, born from above, the beloved of the Father. As a son, the Father is engaged to provide my every need. As a son, I live in dependence and trust, in love and obedience, in joy and hope. It is when I live with the Father as a son, that it becomes possible to make any sacrifice and to obey every command.

Believer! take time and prayer to understand this truth, and let it exercise its full power in your soul. Let the Holy Spirit write it into your innermost being, that you are "predestinate to be conformed to the image of His Son." The Father's object was the honor of His Son, "that He might be the firstborn among many brethren" (Romans 8:29). Let this be your object, too, in all your life—to show forth the image of your Elder Brother, that other Christians may be pointed to Him alone, may praise Him alone, and seek to follow Him more closely, too.

Let it be the fixed and only purpose of your life, the great object of your believing prayer, that "Christ shall be magnified in my body" (Philippians 1:20). This will give you new confidence to ask and expect all that is necessary to live like Christ. Your conformity to Christ will be one of the links connecting the eternal purpose of the Father with the eternal fulfillment of it in the glorifying of the Son. Your conformity to Christ then becomes such a holy, heavenly, divine work, that you realize that it can come only from the Father. From Him, you can and will most certainly receive it. What God's purpose has decreed, God's power will perform. What God's love has ordained and commanded, God's love will most certainly accomplish. A living faith in His eternal purpose will become one of the mightiest powers in urging and helping us to live *Like Christ.*

O incomprehensible Being, I bow before You in deepest humility. It has been such a strength to know that Your Son has chosen me, in order to send me into the world as You had sent Him. But, here You have led me still higher, and shown that this mission to be as He was in the world was from eternity decreed by Yourself. O my God, my soul bows prostrate in the dust before You.

Lord God, now that Your child comes to You for the fulfillment of Your own purpose, he dares to confidently look for an answer. Your will is stronger than every hindrance. The faith that trusts You will not be put to shame. Lord, in holy reverence and worship, but with childlike confidence and hope, I utter this prayer: Father, give me the desire of my soul—conformity to the image of Your Son. Father, likeness to Jesus, this is what my soul desires of You. Let me, like Him, be Your holy child.

O my Father, write it in Your book of remembrance, and write it in my remembrance, too, that I have asked it of You as what I desire above all things, conformity to the image of Your Son.

Father, to this You have chosen me. You will give it to me, to Your own and His glory. Amen.

Chapter 12

LIKE CHRIST...
In Doing God's Will

"For I came down from heaven, not to do my own will, but the will of him that sent me"—John 6:38.

In the will of God we have the highest expression of His divine perfection, and at the same time the high energy of His divine power. Creation owes its being and its beauty to this. It is the manifestation of God's will. In all nature, the will of God is done. In heaven, the angels find their highest blessedness in doing God's will. For this man was created with a free will, so that he might have the power to choose, and, of his own accord, do God's will. And, deceived by the devil, man committed the great sin of doing his own rather than God's will. *Yes, his own rather than God's will!* In this is the root and the wretchedness of sin.

Jesus Christ became man to bring us back to the blessedness of *doing God's will.* The great object of redemption was to make us and our will free from the power of sin, and to lead us again to live and do the will of God. In His life on earth, He showed us what it is to live only for the will of God. In His death and resurrection, He won for us the power to live and do the will of God as He had done.

"Lo, I come to do Thy will, O God" (Hebrews 10:9). These words, uttered through the Holy Spirit by the mouth of one of His prophets long ages before Christ's birth, are the key to His life on earth. At Nazareth in the carpenter's shop, at the Jordan with John the Baptist, in the wilderness with Satan, in public with the multitude, in living and dying, it was this which inspired, guided, and gladdened Him. The glorious will of the Father was to be accomplished in Him and by Him.

We must not think that this cost Him nothing. He says repeatedly, "*Not my will,* but the will of the Father," to let us understand that there was in very deed a denial of His own will. In Gethsemane, the sacrifice of His own will reached its height, but what took place there was only the perfect expression of what had rendered His whole life acceptable to the Father. That man has a will other than God's, is not sin. It is when he clings to his own will when it is seen to be contrary to the will of the Creator that sin occurs. As man, Jesus had a human will, the natural, though not sinful desires which belong to human nature. As man, He did not always know beforehand what the will of God was. He had to wait, be taught of God, and learn from time to time what that will was. But, when the will of His Father was known to Him, then He was always ready to give up His own human will and do the will of the Father. It was this that constituted the perfection and the value of His self-sacrifice. He had once and for all surrendered Himself as a man, to live only in and for the will of God. He was always ready, even to the sacrifice of Gethsemane and Calvary, to do that will alone.

It is *this life of obedience*, worked out by the Lord Jesus in the flesh, that is not only imputed to us, but *imparted through the Holy Spirit.* Through His death, our Lord Jesus has atoned for our self-will and disobedience. It was by conquering it in His own perfect obedience that He atoned for it. He has thus not only blotted out the guilt of our self-will before God, but broken its power in us. In His resurrection, He brought from the dead a life that had conquered and destroyed all self-will. And the believer who knows the power of Jesus' death and resurrection has the power to consecrate himself entirely to God's will. He knows that the call to follow Christ means nothing less than to take and speak the words of the Master as his own solemn vow, "I seek not My own will, but the will of the Father."

To attain this, we must begin by taking the same stand that our Lord did. Take God's will as one great whole, as the only thing for which you live on earth. Look at the sun and moon, the grass and flowers, and see what glory each of them has only because it is doing God's will. But, they do it without knowing it. You can do it still more gloriously, because you knowingly and willingly do it. Let your heart be filled with the thought of the glory of God's will concerning His children, and concerning yourself. Say that it is one purpose that that will should be done in You. Yield yourself to the Father frequently and distinctly, with the declaration that with you, as with Jesus, it is a settled thing that His beautiful and blessed will must and will be done. Say it frequently in your quiet meditations, with a joyful and trusting heart: *Praise God! I may live only to do the will of God.*

Let no fear keep us back from this. Do not think that this will is too hard for us to do. God's will only seems hard as long as we look at it from a distance, and are unwilling to submit to it. Just look again at how beautiful the will of God makes everything in nature. Ask yourself, now that He loves and blesses you as a child, if it is right to distrust Him. The will of God is the will of His love. How can you fear to surrender yourself to it?

Nor let the fear that you will not be able to obey that will keep you back. The Son of God came on earth to show what the life of man must and may become. His resurrection life gives us power to live as He lived. Jesus Christ enables us, through His Spirit, to walk not after the flesh, but according to the will of God.

"I come to do Thy will, O God." Even before the Lord Jesus came to earth, a believer in the Old Testament was able, through the Spirit, to speak that word himself as well as for Christ. Christ took it up and filled it with new life-power. And now, He expects his redeemed ones, since He has been on earth, to even more heartily and entirely make it their choice. Let us do so. We must not first try and see whether, in single instances, we succeed in doing God's will, in the hope of afterwards attaining to the entire consecration that can say: "I come to do Thy will." No, this is not the right way.

Let us first recognize God's will as a whole, the claims it has upon us, as well as its blessedness and glory. Let us surrender ourselves to it as to God Himself. Let us consider it one of the first articles of our creed: I am in the world, like Christ, only to do the Father's will. This surrender will teach us to joyfully accept every command and every providence as part of the will we have already yielded ourselves to. This surrender will give us courage to wait for God's sure guidance and strength, because the man who lives only for God's will may depend on God for his judgment. This surrender will lead us deeper into the consciousness of our utter weakness. It also leads us deeper into the fellowship and the likeness of the beloved Son, and makes us partakers of all the blessedness and love that the Son has prepared for us. There is nothing that will bring us closer to God in union to Christ than loving and keeping and doing the will of God.

Child of God! one of the first marks of conformity to Christ is obedience—simple and implicit obedience to all the will of God. Let it be the most marked thing in your life. Begin by a willing and whole-hearted keeping of every one of the commands of God's holy Word. Go on to a very tender yielding to everything that your conscience tells you is right, even when the Word does not directly command it. In this way, you will rise higher. A hearty obedience to the commandments, as far as you know them, and a ready obedience to conscience wherever it speaks, are the preparation for that divine teaching of the Spirit which will lead you deeper into the meaning and application of the Word. You will gain more direct and spiritual insight into God's will with regard to yourself personally. It is to those *who obey* Him that God gives the Holy Spirit, through whom the blessed will of God becomes the light that continually shines more brightly on our path. "If any man *will do His will,* he shall know" (John 7:17). Blessed will of God! blessed obedience to God's will! oh that we knew to count and keep these as our most precious treasures!

And if it ever appears too hard to live only for God's will, let us remember wherein Christ found His strength: it was because it was *the Father's* will that the Son rejoiced to do it. "This commandment have I received *of My Father"* (John 10:18). This made even the laying down of His life possible. Our union to Jesus, and our calling to live like Him, constantly point us to *His Sonship* as the secret of His life and strength. Let it be our chief desire to say each day, "I am the Father's beloved child," and to think of each commandment as *the Father's* will. A Christlike sense of sonship will lead to a Christlike obedience.

O my God, I thank You for this wondrous gift—Your Son become man—to teach us how man may do the will of his God. I thank You for the glorious calling to be like Him in this, too, with Him to taste the blessedness of a life in perfect harmony with Your glorious and perfect will. I thank You for the power given in Christ to do and to bear all that will. I thank You that in this, too, I may be like the first begotten Son.

I come now, O my Father, afresh to take up my calling in childlike, joyous trust and love. Lord, I want to live wholly and only to do Your will. I want to abide in the Word and wait upon the Spirit. I would, like Your Son, live in fellowship with You in prayer, in the firm confidence that You will day by day make me know Your will more clearly. O my Father, let my desire be acceptable in Your sight. Keep it in the thoughts of my heart forever. Give me grace with true joy continually to say: Not my will, but the will of my Father must be done. I am here on the earth only to do the will of my God. Amen.

Chapter 13

LIKE CHRIST...
In His Compassion

"Then Jesus said, I have compassion on the multitude"—Matthew 15:32.

"Shouldest not thou also have had compassion on thy fellow-servant, even as I had pity on thee?"—Matthew 18:33.

On three different occasions Matthew tells us that our Lord was moved with compassion for the multitude. His whole life was a manifestation of the compassion with which He had looked on the sinner, and of the tenderness with which He was moved at the sight of misery and sorrow. In this, He was the true reflection of our compassionate God, of the father who, moved with compassion toward his prodigal son, fell on his neck and kissed him.

In this compassion of the Lord Jesus, we can see how He did not look upon the will of God He came to do as a duty or an obligation. Instead, He had that divine will dwelling within Him as His own, inspiring and ruling all His sentiments and motives. After He had said, "I came down from heaven, *not to do*

Mine own will, but the will of Him that sent Me," He at once added, "And *this is the Father's will* that of all which He hath given Me I should lose nothing, but should raise it up again at the last day" (John 6:38-39). "And *this is the will* of Him that sent Me, that every one which seeth the Son and believeth on Him, may have everlasting life" (John 6:40). For the Lord Jesus, the will of God consisted not in certain things which were forbidden or commanded. No, He had entered into that which truly forms the very heart of God's will—to lost sinners, He should give eternal life.

Because God Himself is love, His will is that love should have full scope in the salvation of sinners. The Lord Jesus came down to earth in order to manifest and accomplish this will of God. He did not do this as a servant obeying the will of a stranger. In His personal life and all His dispositions, He proved that the loving will of His Father to save sinners was His own. Not only His death on Golgotha, but just as much the compassion in which He took and bore the need of all the wretched, and the tenderness of His fellowship with them, was the proof that the Father's will had truly become His own. In every way, He showed that life was of no value to Him but as the opportunity of doing the will of His Father.

Beloved followers of Christ, who have offered yourselves to imitate Him, let the will of the Father be to you what it was to your Lord. The will of the Father in the mission of His Son was the manifestation and the triumph of divine compassion in the salvation of lost sinners. Jesus could not possibly accomplish this will in any other way than by having and showing this compassion. *God's will is for us what it was for Jesus: the salvation of the perishing.* It is impossible for us to fulfill that will except by having, bearing about, and showing in our lives the compassion of our God. The seeking of God's will must not be only denying ourselves certain things which God forbids, and doing certain works which God commands. It must consist especially in surrendering ourselves to have the same mind and disposition toward sinners as God has, and that we find our pleasure and joy alone in living for this. By the most personal devotion to each poor, perishing sinner around us, and by our helping them in compassionate love, we can show that the will of God is our will. With the compassionate God as our Father, with Christ who was so often moved with compassion as our life, nothing can be more just than the command that the life of every Christian should be one of compassionate love.

Compassion is the spirit of love which is awakened by the sight of need or wretchedness. How many occasions there are for the practice of this heavenly virtue, and what a need there is in a world so full of misery and sin! Every Christian ought, therefore, by prayer and practice, to cultivate a compassionate heart as one of the most precious marks of likeness to the blessed Master. Everlasting love longs to give itself to a perishing world, and to find its satisfaction in saving the lost. *It seeks for vessels which it may fill with the love of God, and send out among the dying that they may drink and live forever.* It asks hearts to be filled with tender compassion at the sight of all the need in which sinners live, hearts that will esteem it their highest blessedness, as the dispensers of God's compassion, to live entirely to bless and save sinners. O my brethren, the everlasting compassion which has had mercy on you calls you, as one who has obtained mercy, to come and let it fill you. It will fit you, in your compassion on all around to be a witness to God's compassionate love.

We have great opportunity to show compassion on all around us. How much there is of temporal want! There are the poor and the sick, widows and orphans, distressed and despondent souls, who need nothing so much as the refreshment a compassionate heart can bring. They live in the midst of Christians, and sometimes complain that it seems as if there are children of the world who have more sympathy than those who are only concerned about their own salvation. O brethren, pray earnestly for a compassionate heart, always on the lookout for an opportunity of doing some work of love, always ready to be an instrument of the divine compassion. It was the compassionate sympathy of Jesus that attracted so many to Him on earth. That same compassionate tenderness will still, more than anything, draw souls to you and to your Lord.

And how much of spiritual misery surrounds us on all sides! Here is a poor, rich man. There is a foolish, thoughtless youth. There is again a poor drunkard, or a hopeless unfortunate. Or perhaps none of these, but simply people entirely engulfed in the follies of the world which surround them. How often are words of unloving indifference, harsh judgment, or slothful hopelessness heard concerning all these! The compassionate heart is rare. Compassion looks on the deepest misery as the place prepared for her by God, and is attracted by it. Compassion never wearies, never gives up hope. Compassion will not allow itself to be rejected, for it is the self-denying love of Christ which inspires it.

The Christian does not confine his compassion to his own circle; he has a large heart. His Lord has shown him the whole heathen world as his field of labor. He seeks to be acquainted with the circumstances of the heathen. He carries their burden on his heart; he is really moved with compassion, and means to help them. Whether the heathenism is near or far off, whether he witnesses it in all its filth and degradation, or only hears of it, compassionate love lives only to accomplish God's will in saving the perishing.

Like Christ in His compassion: let this now be our motto. After uttering the parable of the compassionate Samaritan, who "had compassion," and helped the wounded stranger, the Lord said, "Go and do thou likewise" (Luke 10:33,37). He is Himself the compassionate Samaritan, who speaks to every one of us whom He has saved, "Go and do likewise." Even as I have done to you, do ye likewise. We who owe everything to His compassion, who profess ourselves His followers, who walk in His footsteps and bear His image, oh, let us exhibit His compassion to the world. We can do it. He lives in us; His Spirit works in us. Let us with much prayer and firm faith look to *His example* as the *sure promise* of what we can be. It will be to Him an unspeakable joy, if He finds us prepared for it, not only to show His compassion to us, but through us to the world. And, ours will be the unutterable joy of having a Christlike heart, full of compassion and of great mercy.

O my Lord! my calling is becoming almost too high. In Your compassionate love, too, I must follow and imitate and reproduce Your life. In the compassion wherewith I see and help every bodily and spiritual misery, in the gentle, tender love wherewith every sinner feels that I long to bless men, must the world form some idea of Your compassion. Most merciful One! forgive me that the world has seen so little of it in me. Most mighty Redeemer! let Your compassion not only save me, but so take hold of me and dwell in me that compassion may be the very breath and joy of my life. May Your compassion toward me be within me a living fountain of compassion toward others.

Lord Jesus, I know You can only give this on one condition, that I let go of my own life and my efforts to keep and sanctify that life, and allow You to live in me, to be my life. Most merciful One, I yield myself to You! You have a right to me, You alone.

There is nothing more precious to me than Your compassionate countenance. What can be more blessed than to be like You?

Lord, here I am. I have faith in You, that You will teach and prepare me to obey Your word: "Thou shouldest have had compassion, even as I had compassion on thee." In that faith, I go out this very day to find in my fellowship with others the opportunity of showing how You have loved me. In that faith, it will become the great object of my life to win men to You. Amen.

Chapter 14

LIKE CHRIST...
In His Oneness With The Father

"Holy Father, keep through thine own name those whom thou hast given me, that they may be one, even as we are....That they all may be one; as thou, Father, art in me, and I in thee, that they also may be one in us: that the world may believe that thou hast sent me. And the glory which thou gavest me I have given them; that they may be one, even as we are one. I in them, and thou in me, that they may be made perfect in one; and that the world may know that thou hast sent me, and hast loved them, even as thou hast loved me"—John 17:11,21-23.

What an unspeakable treasure we have in this high-priestly prayer! There, the heart of Jesus is laid open to our view, and we see what His love desires for us. There, the heavens are opened to us, and we learn what He as our Intercessor is continually asking and obtaining for us from the Father.

In that prayer, the mutual union of believers is more important than anything else. In His prayer for all who will in the future believe, this is the chief petition, verses 20-26. He repeats this prayer for their unity three times.

The Lord tells us plainly why He desires it so strongly. *This unity is the only convincing proof to the world that the Father had sent Him.* With all its blindness, the world knows that selfishness is the curse of sin. It is little help that God's children tell that they are born again, that they are happy, that they can do wonders in Jesus' name, or that they can prove that what the Scriptures teach is the truth. When the world sees a Church from which selfishness is banished, then it will acknowledge the divine mission of Christ, because He has worked such a wonder—a community of men who truly and heartily love one another.

The Lord speaks of this unity three times as the reflection of His own oneness with the Father. He knew that this was the perfection of the Godhead: the Father and Son, as separate persons, and yet perfectly one in the living fellowship of the Holy Spirit. And, He cannot imagine anything higher than this, that His believing people should with Him and in Him be one with each other, even as He and the Father are one.

The intercession of the Lord Jesus avails much; it is all-prevailing. What He asks, He receives of His Father. But lo! the blessing which descends finds no entrance in hearts where there is no open door, no place prepared, to receive it. How many believers do not even desire to be one even as the Father and the Son are one! They are so accustomed to a life of selfishness and imperfect love that they do not even long for such perfect love. They put off that union until they meet in heaven. And yet, the Lord was thinking of life on earth when He twice said, "That the world may know."

That "they may be one even as we are one." The Church must be awakened to understand and to value this prayer properly. This union is one of life and love at once. Some explain it as referring to the hidden life-union which binds all believers, even under external divisions. But, this is not what the Lord means. He speaks of something that the world can see, something that resembles the union between God the Father and God the Son. The hidden unity of life must be manifest in the visible unity and fellowship of love. Only when it becomes impossible for believers, in the different smaller circles in which they are associated, not to live in the full oneness of love with the children of God around them will the possibility of oneness be fully realized. Only when they learn that a life in love to each other, such as Christ's to us, and the Father's to Him, is simple duty, and begin to cry to God for His Holy Spirit to work it in them, only then will there be hope of change in this respect. The fire will spread from circle to circle and from church to church, until all who truly do the will of God will consecrate themselves to abide in love, even as God is love.

And what are we to do now, while we wait for and wish to hasten that day? Let everyone who earnestly takes up the word of the Master, "Even as I, so also ye," begin with his own circle of friends. And in that circle, let him begin with himself first. However weak or sickly, however perverse or trying the members of Christ's body may be with whom he is surrounded, let him live with them in close fellowship and love. Whether they are willing for it or not, whether they accept or reject, let him love them with a Christlike love. Yes, to love them as Christ does must be the purpose of his life. This love will find an echo in some hearts at least, and will awaken in them the desire to seek the life of love and perfect oneness as well.

But what discoveries such effort will bring of the inability of the believer, who has thus far been satisfied with the ordinary Christian life, to reach this standard! He will soon find that nothing will avail but a personal, undivided consecration. To have a love like Christ's, I must truly have a life like Christ's. *I must live with His life.* This lesson must be relearned: Christ in the fullest sense of the word will be the life of those who dare to trust Him for it. Those who cannot trust with a full trust, cannot love with a full love.

Believer, listen once more to the simple way to such a life. First of all, acknowledge your calling to live and love just like Christ. Confess your inability to fulfill this calling, even in the very least. Listen to the word that Christ is waiting to prepare you to fulfill this calling, if you will give yourself unreservedly to Him. Make the surrender in this, that conscious of being utterly unable to do anything in your own strength, you offer yourself to your Lord to work in you both to will and to do. And then count most confidently on Him, who in the power of His unceasing intercession can save completely, to work in you what He has asked of His Father for you. Yes, count on Him who has said to the Father, "Thou in Me and I in them, that they may be one, even as we are one." He will manifest His life in you with heavenly power. As you live with His life, you will love with His love.

Beloved fellow Christians, the oneness of Christ with the Father is our model: even as they, so must we be one. Let us love one another, serve one another, bear with one another, help one another, and live for one another. For our love is too small: but we will earnestly pray that Christ give us His love wherewith to love. With God's love shed abroad in our hearts through the Holy Spirit, we will be so one that the world will know that it is indeed the truth, that the Father sent Christ into the world, and that Christ has given in us the very life and love of heaven.

Holy Father, we know now with what petitions He, who lives to make constant intercession, continually approaches You. It is for the perfect unity of His disciples. Father, we, too, cry to You for this blessing. Alas, how divided the Church is! It is not the division of language or country that we deplore, not even the difference of doctrine or teaching that so much grieves us, but, Lord! the want of that unity of spirit and love whereby Your Church should convince the world that she is from heaven.

O Lord! we desire to confess before You with deep shame the coldness, selfishness, distrust, and bitterness that is still at times to be seen among Your children. We confess before You our own want of that fervent and perfect love to which You have called us. O forgive, and have mercy upon us.

Lord God! visit Your people. It is through the one Spirit that we can know and show our unity in the one Lord. Let the Holy Spirit work powerfully in Your believing people to make them one. Let it be felt in every circle where God's children meet each other, how indispensable a close union in the love of Jesus is. And let my heart, too, be delivered from self, to realize, in the fellowship with Your children, how we are one, even as You, Father, and Your Son are one. Amen.

Chapter 15

LIKE CHRIST...
In His Dependence On The Father

"Verily, verily, I say unto you, The Son can do nothing of himself, but what he seeth the Father do: for what things soever he doeth, these also doeth the Son likewise. For the Father loveth the Son, and sheweth him all things that himself doeth: and he will shew him greater works than these, that ye may marvel"—John 5:19-20.

"I know my sheep, and am known of mine. As the Father knoweth me, even so know I the Father"—John 10:14-15.

Our relationship to Jesus is the exact counterpart of His to the Father. And so, the words in which He sets forth His communion with the Father have their truth in us, too. And as the words of Jesus in John 5 describe the natural relationship between every father and son, whether on earth or in heaven, they are applicable not only to the Only-begotten, but to everyone who, in and like Jesus, is called a son of God.

There is no better way to think of the simple truth

and force of the illustration than by thinking of Jesus learning His trade from His earthly father in the carpenter's shop. The first thing you notice is the entire *dependence:* "The son can do nothing of himself, but what he seeth the father do." Then you are struck by the implicit *obedience* that just seeks to imitate the father: "for what things soever (the father) doeth, these also doeth the son likewise." You then notice the loving *intimacy* to which the father admits him, keeping back none of his secrets: "for the father loveth the son, and sheweth him all things that himself doeth." And, in this dependent obedience on his son's part, and the loving teaching on the father's part, you have the pledge of an ever-growing *advance* to greater works. Step by step, the son will be led up to all that the father himself can do: "He will shew him greater works than these, that ye may marvel."

In this picture, we have the reflection of the relationship between God the Father and the Son in His blessed humanity. If His human nature is to be something real and true, and if we are to understand how Christ is in very deed to be our example, we must fully believe in what our blessed Lord here reveals to us of the secrets of His inner life. The words He speaks are literal truth. His dependence on the Father for each moment of His life was absolutely and intensely real: "The Son can do nothing of Himself, but what He seeth the Father do." He counted it no humiliation to wait on Him for His commands. He rather considered it His highest blessedness to let Himself be led and guided by the Father as a child. And accordingly, He held Himself bound in strictest obedience to say and do only what the Father showed Him: "What things soever (the Father) doeth, these also doeth the Son likewise."

The proof of this is the exceeding carefulness with which He always seeks to keep to Holy Scripture. In His sufferings, He will endure all so that the Scriptures may be fulfilled. For this, He remained the whole night in prayer. In such continued prayer, He presents His thoughts to the Father, and waits for the answer, that He may know the Father's will. No child in his ignorance, no slave in his bondange, was ever so anxious to keep to what the father or master had said as the Lord Jesus was to follow the teaching and guidance of His heavenly Father. On this account, the Father kept nothing hid from Him. His entire dependence and willingness to always learn were rewarded with the most perfect communication of all the Father's secrets. "For the Father loveth the Son, and sheweth Him all things...and He will shew Him greater works than these, that ye may marvel." The Father had formed a glorious life plan for the Son, that in Him the divine life might be shown forth in the conditions of human existence. This plan was shown to the Son piece by piece until at last all was gloriously accomplished.

Child of God, it is not only for the only-begotten Son that a life plan has been arranged, but for each one of His children. Just in proportion to how we live in more or less entire dependence on the Father will this life plan be more or less perfectly worked out in our lives. The nearer the believer comes to this entire dependence of the Son, "doing nothing but what He sees the Father do," and then to His implicit obedience, "what things soever He doeth, these also doeth likewise," so much more will the promise be fulfilled to us: "The Father sheweth Him all things that He Himself doeth, and He will shew Him greater works than these." Like Christ! that word calls us to a life of conformity to the Son in His blessed dependence on the Father. Each one of us is invited to thus live.

To such a life of dependence on the Father, the first thing that is necessary is a firm faith that He will make His will known to us. I think this is something that keeps many back: they cannot believe that the Lord cares for them so much that He will indeed take the trouble to teach them and to make His will known to them, just as He did to Jesus. Christian, you are of more value to the Father than you know. You are worth the price He paid for you—that is, the blood of His Son. He, therefore, attaches the highest value to the least thing that concerns you, and will guide you even in what is most insignificant. He longs for close and constant fellowship with you more than you can conceive. He can use you for His glory, and make something of you, higher than you can understand. The Father loves His child, and shows him what He does. That He proved in Jesus; and He will prove it in us, too. There must only be the surrender to expect His teaching. Through His

Holy Spirit He gives this most tenderly. Without removing us from our circle, the Father can so conform us to Christ's image that we can be a blessing and joy to all. Do not let unbelief of God's compassionate love prevent us from expecting the Father's guidance in all things.

Do not let the unwillingness to submit yourself keep you back either. This is the second great hindrance. The desire for independence was the temptation in paradise, and is the temptation in each human heart. It seems hard to be nothing, to know nothing, to will nothing. And yet, it is so blessed. This dependence brings us into most blessed communion with God. It becomes true of us as it did of Jesus, "The Father loveth the Son, and sheweth Him all things that Himself doeth." This dependence takes from us all care and responsibility: we have only to obey orders. It gives real power and strength of will, because we know that He works in us to will and to do. It gives us the blessed assurance that our work will succeed, because we have allowed God alone to take charge of it.

My brethren, if you have so far only known a little about this life of conscious dependence and simple obedience, begin today. Let your Savior be your example in this. It is His blessed will to live in you, and in you to be again what He was here on earth. He only longs for your acquiesence: He will work it in you. Offer yourself to the Father this day, after the example of the First-begotten, to do nothing of yourself but only what the Father shows you. Fix your gaze on Jesus as the Example and Promise of what you will be. Adore Him who, for your sake, humbled Himself, and showed how blessed the dependent life can be.

Blessed dependence! it is indeed the disposition which becomes us toward such a God. It gives Him the glory which belongs to Him as God. It keeps the soul in peace and rest, for it allows God to care for all. It keeps the mind quiet and prepared to receive and use the Father's teaching. And, it is so gloriously rewarded in the deeper experience of holy fellowship, and the continued, ever-advancing discoveries of His will and work with which the Father crowns it. Blessed dependence! in which the Son lived on earth, is the desire of my soul.

Blessed dependence! it was because Jesus knew that He was *a Son* that He thus loved to be dependent on *the Father.* Of all the teaching in regard to the likeness to Christ, this is the center and sum: I must live as a Son with my Father. If I stand clear in this relationship, *as a son realizing that the Father is everything to me,* a sonlike life, living through the Father, living for the Father, will be its natural and spontaneous outcome.

O my Father, the longer I fix my gaze upon the image of the Son, the more I discover the fearful ruin of my nature, and how far sin has estranged me from You. To be dependent upon You: there can be no higher blessedness than this; to trust in all things in a God such as You are, so wise and good, so rich and powerful. And lo! it has become the most difficult thing there can be. We would rather be dependent on our own folly than the God of all glory. Even Your own children, O most blessed Father! often think it so hard to give up their own thoughts and will, and to believe that absolute dependence on God, to the very least of things, is alone true blessedness.

Lord! I come to You with the humble prayer: teach me this. He who purchased, with His own blood, for me the everlasting blessedness, has shown me in His own life wherein that blessedness consists. And, I know He will now lead and keep me in it. O my Father! in Your Son I yield myself to You, to be made like Him, like Him to do nothing of myself, but what I see the Father do. Father! You will even take me, like the Firstborn, and for His sake, into Your training, and show me what You do. O my God! be a Father unto me as unto Christ, and let me be Your son, as He was. Amen.

Chapter 16

LIKE CHRIST . . .
In His Love

"A new commandment I give unto you, That ye love one another; as I have loved you, that ye also love one another"—John 13:34.

"This is my commandment, That ye love one another, as I have loved you"—John 15:12.

It is not the command of a law which convinces us of sin and weakness; it is a new command under a new covenant, that is established upon better promises. It is the command of Him who asks nothing that He has not provided, and now offers to bestow. It is the assurance that He expects nothing from us, that He does not work in us. As I have loved you, and every moment am pouring out that love on you through the Holy Spirit, even so, love one another. The measure, the strength, and the work of your love will be found in My love to you.

As I have loved you: that word gives us the *measure* of the love with which we must love each other. True love knows no measure: it gives itself entirely. It may take the time and measure of showing it into consideration, but love itself is ever whole and undivided. This is the greatest glory of divine love that we have—the Father and Son, two persons, who, in love, remain One Being, each losing Himself in the other. This is the glory of the love of Jesus, who is the image of God, that He loves us as the Father loves Him. And, this is the glory of brotherly love, that it will know of no other law than to love as God and Christ.

He who desires to be like Christ must unhesitatingly accept this as his rule of life. He knows how difficult, how impossible it often is to thus love brethren, in whom there often is so much that is offensive or unamiable. Before going out to meet them in circumstances where his love may be tried, he goes in secret to the Lord. With his eye fixed on his own sin and unworthiness, he asks: How much do you owe your Lord? He goes to the cross and seeks to fathom the love with which the Lord has loved him. He lets the light of the immeasurable love of Him who is in heaven—his Head and his Brother—shine in on his soul, until he learns to feel that divine love has only one law: love seeks not its own; love gives itself wholly. And, he lays himself on the altar before his Lord: even as You have loved me, so will I love the brethren. In virtue of my union with Jesus and in Jesus with them, there can be no question of anything less: I love them as Christ did. Oh, that Christians would close there ears to all the reasonings of their own hearts, and fix their eyes only on the law which He who loves them has emulated in His own example. Then, they would realize that there is nothing for them to do but this—to accept His commands and to obey them.

Our love may recognize no other measure than His, because His love is *the strength* of ours. The love of Christ is no mere idea or sentiment. It is a real, divine life power. As long as the Christian does not understand this, it cannot exert its full power in him. But, when his faith rises to realize that Christ's love is nothing less than the imparting of Himself and His love to the beloved, and he becomes rooted in this love as the source from which his life derives its sustenance, then he sees that his Lord simply asks that he allow His love to flow through him. He must live in a Christ-given strength. The love of Christ constrains him, and enables him to love as He did.

From this love of Christ, the Christian also learns what the work of his love to the brethren must be. We have already had occasion to speak of many manifestations of love—its loving service, its self-denial, its meekness. Love is the root of all these. It teaches the disciple to look upon himself as really called to be, in his little circle, just like Jesus, the one who lives solely to love and help others. Paul prays for the Philippians: "That your love may abound yet more and more in knowledge and in all judgement" (Philippians 1:9). Love does not at once comprehend the work that it can do. The believer who prays that his love may abound in knowledge, and really takes Christ's example as his rule of life, will be taught what a great and glorious work there is for him to do. The Church of God, and every child of God as well as the world, has an unspeakable need of love—of the manifestation of Christ's love. The Christian who really takes the Lord's word, "Love one another, as I have loved you," as a command that must be obeyed, carries about a power for blessing and life for all those he comes in contact with. Love is the explanation of the whole wonderful life of Christ, and of the wonder of His death. Divine love in God's children will still work its mighty wonders.

"Behold, what manner of love!" (1 John 3:1). "Behold how He loved!" (John 11:36). These words are the superscription over the love of the Father and of the Son. They must yet become the keywords to the life of every Christian. They will be so where, in living faith and true consecration, the command of Christ to love, as He loved, is accepted as the law of life. As early as the call of Abraham, this principle was deposited as a living seed in God's Kingdom, that what God is for us, we must be for others. "I will bless thee," and "thou shalt be a blessing" (Genesis 12:2). If "I have loved you" is the highest manifestation of what God is for us, then "Even so love ye" must be the first and highest expression of what the child of God must be. In preaching, as in the life of the Church, it must be understood: *The love which loves like Christ is the sign of true discipleship.*

Beloved Christians! Christ Jesus longs for you in order to make you, amid those who surround you, a very fountain of love. The love of heaven would gladly take possession of you, so that, in and through you, it may work its blessed work on earth. Yield to its rule. Offer yourself unreservedly to its indwelling. Honor it by the confident assurance that it can teach you to love as Jesus loved. As conformity to the Lord Jesus must be the chief mark of your Christian walk, so love must be the chief mark of that conformity. Do not be disheartened if you do not attain it at once. Only keep a firm hold of the command, "Love, as I have loved you." It takes time to grow into it. Take time in secret to gaze on that image of love. Take time in prayer and meditation to fan the desire for it into a burning flame. Take time to survey all around you, whoever they may be, and whatever may happen, with this one thought, "I must love them." Take time to become conscious of your union with your Lord, that every fear as to the possibility of thus loving may be met with the word: "Have not I commanded you: Love as I have loved"? Christian, take time in loving communion with Jesus, your loving example, and you will joyfully fulfill this command, too, to love as He did.

Lord Jesus, who has loved me so wonderfully, and now commands me to love even as You, behold me at Your feet. Joyfully, I accept Your commands, and now go out in Your strength to manifest Your love to all.

In your strength, O my Lord! Therefore, be pleased to reveal Your love to me. Shed abroad Your love in my heart through the Holy Spirit. Let me live each moment in the experience that I am the beloved of God.

Lord, let me understand that I can love, not with my own, but with Your love. You live in me; Your Spirit dwells and works in me. From You, there streams into me the love with which I can love others. You only ask that I understand and accept my calling, and that I surrender myself to live as You did. You want me to look on my old nature with its selfish and unlovingness as crucified, and in faith prepare to do as You command.

Lord, I do it. In the strength of my Lord, I want to live *to love even as You have loved me.* Amen.

Chapter 17

LIKE CHRIST...
In His Praying

"And in the morning, rising up a great while before day, he went out, and departed into a solitary place, and there prayed"—Mark 1:35.

"And he saith unto them, Come ye yourselves apart into a desert place, and rest a while"—Mark 6:31.

In His life of secret prayer, too, my Savior is my example. He could not maintain the heavenly life in His soul without continually separating Himself from man, and communing with His Father. The heavenly life in me has the same need of entire separation from man—the need not only of single moments, but of time enough for fellowship with the Fountain of Life, the Father in heaven.

The event which so attracted the attention of His disciples happened at the beginning of His public ministry, and they wrote it down. After a day full of wonders and of work at Capernaum (Mark 1:21-32), the crowd in the evening became still greater. The whole town is before the door, sick are healed, and devils are cast out. It is late before they get to sleep. In the throng, there is little time for quiet or for secret prayer. And, as they rise early in the morning, they find Him gone. In the silence of the night, He has gone out to seek a place of solitude in the wilderness. When they find Him there, He is still praying.

And why did my Savior need these hours of prayer? Did He not know the blessedness of silently lifting up His soul to God in the midst of the most pressing business? Did the Father not dwell in Him? And did He not, in the depth of His heart, enjoy unbroken communion with Him? Yes, that hidden life was indeed His portion. But that life, as subject to the law of humanity, had need of continual refreshing and renewing from the fountain. It was a life of dependence. Just because it was strong and true, it could not bear the loss of direct and constant communion with the Father, with whom and in whom it had its being and its blessedness.

What a lesson for every Christian! Much fellowship with man is dissipating and dangerous to our spiritual life. It brings us under the influence of the visible and temporal. Nothing can atone for the loss of secret and direct communion with God. Even work in the service of God and of love is exhausting. We cannot bless others without power going out from us, and this must be renewed from above. The law of the manna—that what is heavenly cannot remain good long upon earth, but must daily be renewed afresh from heaven—still holds true. Jesus Christ teaches it to us: I need every day to have communion with my Father in secret. My life is like His, a life hid in heaven, in God. It needs time day by day to be fed from heaven. It is *from heaven* alone that the power to lead *a heavenly life* on earth can come.

And what may have been the prayers that occupied our Lord there so long? If I could hear Him pray, how I might learn how I too must pray! God be praised! We have more than one of His prayers recorded, that in them, we might learn to follow His holy example. In the high-priestly prayer (John 17) we hear Him speak, as in the deep calm of heaven, to His Father. In His Gethsemane prayer, a few hours later, we see Him call out of the depths of trouble and darkness unto God. In these two prayers we have all: the highest and the deepest there is to be found in the communion of prayer between Father and Son.

In both these prayers, we see how He addresses God. Each time it is *Father! O my Father!* In that word lies the secret of all prayer. The Lord knew that He was a Son, and that the Father loved Him. With that word, He placed Himself in the full light of the Father's countenance. This was to Him the greatest need and greatest blessing of prayer—to enter into the full enjoyment of the Father's love. Let it be thus with me, too. Let the principle part of my prayer be the holy silence and adoration of faith, in which I wait on God until He reveals Himself to me, and gives me, through His Spirit, the loving assurance that He looks down on me as a Father—that I am well pleasing to Him.

He who, in prayer, does not have time in quietness of soul, and in full consciousness of its meaning to say Abba Father, has missed the best part of prayer. It is in prayer that the witness of the Spirit—that we are children of God and that the Father draws nigh and delights in us—must be exercised and strengthened.. "If our heart condemn us not, then we have confidence toward God. And whatsoever we ask, we receive of Him, because we obey His commandments, and do the things that are pleasing in His sight" (1 John 3:21).

In both these prayers, I also see what He desired: *that the Father may be glorified.* He speaks: "I have glorified Thee; glorify Thy Son, that Thy Son *also may glorify Thee."* That most assuredly was the spirit of every prayer—the entire surrender of Himself only to live for the Father's will and glory. All that He asked had only one object, "That God might be glorified." In this, too, He is my example. I must seek to have the spirit of each prayer I offer: Father! bless Your child, and glorify Your grace in me, only so that I may glorify You. Everything in the universe must show forth God's glory. The Christian who is inspired with this thought, and avails himself of prayer to express it until he is thoroughly imbued with it, will have power in prayer. Even of His work in heaven our Lord says: "Whatsoever ye shall ask in My name, that will I do, *that the Father may be glorified in the Son"* (John 14:13). O my soul, learn from your Savior, before you pour out your desires in prayer, first to yield yourself as a whole burnt offering, with the one object that God may be glorified in you.

Then, you have sure ground on which to pray. You will feel the strong desire, as well as the full liberty, to ask the Father that in each part of Christ's example—in each feature of Christ's image—you may be made like Him, so that God may be glorified. You will understand how, only in continually renewed prayer, the soul can surrender itself to wait for God to work in it what will be to His glory. Because Jesus surrendered Himself so entirely to the glory of His Father, He was worthy to be our Mediator. He could, in His high-priestly prayer, ask such great blessings for His people. Learn like Jesus to seek only God's glory in prayer, and you will become a true intercessor, who can not only approach the throne of grace with his own needs, but can also pray for others the effectual, fervent prayer of a righteous man that avails much. The words which the Savior put into our mouth in the Lord's Prayer: "Thy will be done," because He was made like His brethren in all things, He took from our lips again and make His own in Gethsemane. In that way, we might receive them back again, in the power of His atonement and intercession, and so be able to pray them even as He had done. You, too, will become Christlike in that priestly intercession, on which the unity and prosperity of the Church and the salvation of sinners so much depend.

And he who in every prayer makes God's glory the

chief object will also, if God calls him to it, have strength for the prayer of Gethsemane. Every prayer of Christ was intercession because He had given Himself for us. All He asked and received was in our interest. Every prayer He prayed was in the spirit of self-sacrifice. Give yourself, too, wholly to God for man, and, as with Jesus, so with us, the entire sacrifice of ourselves to God in every prayer of daily life is the only preparation for those single hours of soul struggle in which we may be called to some special act of the surrender of the will that costs us tears and anguish. But, he who has learned the former will surely receive strength for the latter.

O my brethren! if you and I want to be like Jesus, we must especially contemplate Jesus praying alone in the wilderness. *There is the secret of His wonderful life*. What He did and spoke to man *was first spoken and lived through with the Father*. In communion with Him, the anointing with the Holy Spirit was each day renewed. He who desires to be like Him in his walk and conversation, must simply begin by following Jesus into solitude. Even though it might cost the sacrifice of night rest, of business, of fellowship with friends, *the time must be found to be alone with the Father*. Besides the ordinary hour of prayer, he will feel, at times, irresistibly drawn to enter into the holy place, and not to come away until it has once again been revealed to him that God is his portion. In his secret chamber, with closed door; or in the solitude of the wilderness, God must be found every day and our fellowship with Him renewed. If

Christ needed it, how much more we! What it was to Him, it will be for us.

What it was to Him is apparent from what is written of His baptism: "It came to pass, that Jesus also being baptized, *and praying*, the heaven was opened, and the Holy Ghost descended in a bodily shape like a dove upon Him; and a voice came from heaven which said, Thou art my beloved Son; in Thee I am well pleased" (Luke 3:21-22). Yes, this will be to us the blessing of prayer: the opened heaven, the baptism of the Spirit, the Father's voice, and the blessed assurance of His love and good pleasure. *As with Jesus, so with us; from above, from above, must it all come in answer to prayer.*

Christlike praying in secret will be the secret of Christlike living in public. O let us rise and avail ourselves of our wonderful privilege—the Christlike boldness of access into the Father's presence, the Christlike liberty with God in prayer.

O my blessed Lord, You have called me, and I have followed You, that I may bear Your image in all things. Daily, I seek Your footsteps, that I may be led by You wherever You go. This day, I have found them, wet with the dew of night, leading to the wilderness. There, I have seen You kneeling for hours before the Father. There, I have heard You, too, in prayer. You gave up all to the Father's glory, and from the Father, You ask, expect, and receive all. Impress, I beseech You, this wonderful vision deep in my soul: my Savior rising up a great while before day to seek communion with His Father, and to ask and obtain in prayer all that He needed for His life and work.

O my Lord! who am I that I may thus listen to You? Yes, who am I that You call me to pray, even as You have done? Precious Savior, from the depths of my heart I beseech You, awaken in me the same strong need of secret prayer. Convince me more deeply that, as with You so with me, the divine life cannot attain its full growth without much secret communion with my heavenly Father, so that my soul may indeed dwell in the light of His countenance. Let this conviction awaken in me such burning desire that I may not rest until each day afresh my soul has been baptized in the streams of heavenly love. O You my Example and Intercessor! teach me to pray like You. Amen.

Chapter 18

LIKE CHRIST...
In His Use Of Scripture

"That all things must be fulfilled, which were written in the law of Moses, and in the prophets, and in the Psalms, concerning me"—Luke 24:44.

What the Lord Jesus accomplished here on earth as man He owed greatly to His use of the Scriptures. In them, He found the way in which He had to walk, the food and the strength on which He could work, and the weapon by which He could overcome every enemy. The Scriptures were indeed indispensable to Him through all His life and passion: from beginning to end His life was the fulfillment of what had been written of Him in the volume of the Book.

It is scarcely necessary to give proof of this. In the temptation in the wilderness, it was by His *"It is written"* that He conquered Satan (Matthew 4:4). In His conflicts with the Pharisees, He continually appealed to the Word: *"What saith the Scripture?" "Have ye not read?" "Is it not written?"* In His fellowship with His disciples it was always from the Scriptures that He proved the certainty and necessity of His sufferings and resurrection: *"How then shall the Scriptures be fulfilled?"* (Matthew 26:54). And in His communion with His Father in His last sufferings, it is in the words of Scripture that He pours out the complaint of being forsaken, and then again commends His spirit into the Father's hands. All this has a very deep meaning. He was Himself the living Word. He had the spirit without measure. If any one could have done without the written Word, it would have been Him. And yet, we see that it is everything to Him. More than any one else, He thus shows us that *the life of God in human flesh and the Word of God in human speech* are inseparably connected. Jesus would not have been what He was, could not have done what He did, had He not yielded Himself step by step to be led and sustained by the Word of God.

Let us try to understand what this teaches us. The Word of God is more than once called Seed; it is the seed of the divine life. We know what seed is. It is that wonderful organism in which the life, the invisible essence of a plant or tree, is so concentrated and embodied that it can be taken away and made available to impart the life of the tree elsewhere. This use may be twofold. As fruit we eat it, for instance, in the corn that gives us bread. The life of the plant becomes our nourishment and our life. Or, we sow it, and the life of the plant reproduces and multiplies itself. In both aspects, the Word of God is seed.

True life is found only in God. But that life cannot be imparted to us unless it is set before us in some shape in which we know and recognize it. It is in the Word of God that the invisible, divine life takes shape, brings itself within our reach, and becomes communicable. The life, the thoughts, the sentiments, and the power of God are embodied in His words. And, it is only through His Word that the life of God can really enter into us. His Word is the seed of the heavenly life.

As the bread of life we eat it, we feed upon it. In eating our daily bread, the body takes in the nourishment which visible nature—the sun and the earth—prepared for us in the seed corn. We assimilate it, and it becomes our very own, part of ourselves; it is our life. In feeding upon the Word of God, the powers of the heavenly life enter into us, and become our very own; we assimilate them. They become a part of ourselves, the life of our life.

Or, we use the seed to plant. The words of God are sown in our heart. They have a divine power of reproduction and multiplication. The very life that is in them, the divine thought, disposition, or powers that each of them contains, takes root in the believing heart and grows up. And, the very thing of which the word was the expression is produced within us. The words of God are the seeds of the fullness of the divine life.

When the Lord Jesus was made man, He became entirely dependent upon the Word of God. He submitted Himself wholly to it. His mother taught it to him. The teachers of Nazareth instructed Him in it. In meditation and prayer, in the exercise of obedience and faith, He was led, during His silent years of preparation, to understand and appropriate it. The Word of the Father was to the Son the life of His soul. What He said in the wilderness was spoken from His innermost personal experience: "Man shall not live by bread alone, but by every word that proceedeth out of the mouth of God" (Matthew 4:4). He felt that He could not live except as the Word brought Him the life of the Father. His whole life was a life of faith, a depending on the Word of the Father. The Word was not a replacement for the Father, but a vehicle for living fellowship with the living God. And, He had His whole mind and heart so filled with it that the Holy Spirit could, at each moment, find within Him, all ready for use, the right word He needed to hear.

Child of God! do you want to become a man of God, strong in faith, full of blessing, rich in fruit to the glory of God, full of the Word of God? Like Christ, make the Word your bread. Let it dwell richly in you. Have your heart full of it. Feed on it. Believe it. Obey it. It is only by believing and obeying that the Word can enter into our inward parts, into our very being. Take it day by day as the Word that proceeds, not has proceeded, but proceeds, is proceeding out of the mouth of God. Regard it as the Word of the living God, who in it holds living fellowship with His children, and speaks to them in living power. Take your thoughts of God's will, God's work, and God's purpose with you and the world—not from the Church, not from Christians around you, but from the Word taught you by the Father—and, like Christ, you will be able to fulfill all that is written in the Scripture concerning you.

In Christ's use of Scripture, the most remarkable thing is this: *He found Himself there. There, He saw His own image and likeness.* And, He gave Himself to the fulfillment of what He found written there. It was this that encouraged Him under the bitterest sufferings, and strengthened Him for the most difficult work. Everywhere, He saw the divine waymark traced by God's own hand: *through suffering to glory.* He had only one thought: to be what the Father had said He should be, to have His life correspond exactly to the image of what He should be as He found it in the Word of God.

Disciple of Jesus, in the Scriptures *your likeness can also be found*—a picture of what the Father means you to be. Seek to have a deep and clear impression of what the Father says in His Word that you should be. Once this is fully understood, it is inconceivable what courage it will give to conquer every difficulty. I have seen what has been written concerning me in God's book. I have seen the image of what I am called in God's counsel to be. Knowing that likeness to Christ is ordained of God inspires my soul with a faith which conquers the world.

The Lord Jesus found His own image not only in the institutions, but especially in the believers of the Old Testament. Moses, Aaron, Joshua, David, and the Prophets were types. And so, He is Himself again the image of believers in the New Testament. It is especially in *Him and His example* that we must find our own image in the Scriptures. To be "changed into the same image from glory to glory, even as by the Spirit of the Lord" (2 Corinthians 3:18), we must in the Scripture-glass gaze on that image as our own. In order to accomplish His work in us, the Spirit teaches us to take Christ as our Example, and to gaze on every feature as the promise of what we can be.

Blessed is the Christian who has truly done this—who has not only found Jesus in the Scriptures, but also in His image the promise and example of what he is to become. Blessed is the Christian who yields himself to be taught, by the Holy Spirit, not to indulge in human thoughts about the Scriptures and what it says of believers, but in simplicity to accept what it reveals of God's thoughts about His children.

Child of God! it was "according to the Scriptures" that Jesus Christ lived and died. It was "according to the Scriptures" that He was raised again. All that the Scriptures said He must do or suffer He was able to accomplish, because He knew and obeyed them. All that the Scripture had promised that the Father would do for Him, the Father did. O give yourself up with an undivided heart to learn in the Scriptures what God says and seeks of you. Let the Scriptures in which Jesus found the food of His life be your daily food and meditation. Go to God's Word each day with the joyful and confident expectation that, through the blessed Spirit who dwells in us, the Word will indeed accomplish its divine purpose in you. Every word of God is full of a divine life and power. Be assured that when you seek to use the Scriptures as Christ used them, they will do for you what they did for Him. God has marked out the plan of your life in His Word. Each day, you will find some portion of it there. Nothing makes a man more strong and courageous than the assurance that he is living out the will of God. God Himself, who had your image portrayed in the Scriptures, will see to it that the Scriptures are fulfilled in you if, like His Son, you will surrender yourself to this as the highest object of your life.

O Lord, my God! I thank You for Your precious Word, the divine glass of all unseen and eternal realities. I thank You that I have in it the image of Your Son, who is Your image, and also, O wonderful grace! my image. I thank You that as I gaze on Him I may also see what I can be.

O my Father! teach me to rightly understand what a blessing Your Word can bring me. To Your Son, when here on earth, it was the manifestation of Your will, the communication of Your life and strength, the fellowship with Yourself. In the acceptance and the surrender to Your Word, He was able to fulfill all Your counsel. May Your Word be all this to me, too. Make it to me, each day afresh through the anointing of the Holy Spirit, the Word proceeding from the mouth of God, the voice of Your living presence speaking to me. May I feel with each word of Yours that it is God coming to impart to me something of

His own life. Teach me to keep it hidden in my heart as a divine seed, which in its own time will spring up and reproduce in me in divine reality the very life that was hid in it—the very thing which I at first only saw in at as a thought. Teach me, above all, O my God, to find in it Him who is its center and substance, Himself the eternal Word. Finding Him, and myself in Him, as my Head and Exemplar, I will learn, like Him, to count Your Word my food and my life.

I ask this, O my God, in the name of our blessed Christ Jesus. Amen.

Chapter 19

LIKE CHRIST...
In Forgiving

"Forbearing one another, and forgiving one another, if any man have a quarrel against any: even as Christ forgave you, so also do ye"—Colossians 3:13.

In the life of grace, forgiveness is one of the first blessings we receive from God. It is also one of the most glorious. It is the transition from the old to the new life—the sign and pledge of God's love. With it, we receive the right to all the spiritual gifts which are prepared for us in Christ. The redeemed saint can never forget, either here or in eternity, that he is a forgiven sinner. Nothing works more mightily to inflame his love, to awaken his joy, or to strengthen his courage than the experience, continually renewed by the Holy Spirit as a living reality, of God's forgiving love. Every day, every thought of God reminds him: I owe all to pardoning grace.

This forgiving love is one of the greatest marvels in the manifestation of the divine nature. In it, God finds His glory and blessedness. And, it is in this glory and blessedness that God wants His redeemed people to share. When He calls upon them, as soon and as much as they have received forgiveness, they are also to bestow it on others.

Have you ever noticed how often and how expressly the Lord Jesus spoke of it? If we thoughtfully read our Lord's words in Matthew 6:12,15; 18:2-25; Mark 11:25, we will understand how inseparably the two are united: God's forgiveness of us and our forgiveness of others. After the Lord was ascended to grant repentance and forgiveness of sins, the Scriptures say of Him just what He had said of the Father, we must forgive like Him. As our text expresses it, *even as Christ* has forgiven you, *so also do ye*. We must be like God, like Christ, in forgiving.

It is not difficult to find the reason for this. When forgiving love comes to us, it is not only to deliver us from punishment. No, much more. It seeks to win us for its own, to take possession of us, and to dwell in us. And when it has thus come down to dwell in us, it does not lose its own heavenly character and beauty. It is still forgiving love seeking to do its work toward us, in us, and through us, leading and enabling us to forgive those who sin against us. So much so is this the case, that we are told that not to forgive is a sure sign that one has himself not been forgiven. He who only seeks forgiveness from selfishness and as freedom from punishment, but has not truly accepted forgiving love to rule his heart and life, proves that God's forgiveness has never really reached him. He who, on the other hand, has really accepted forgiveness, will have in the joy with which he forgives others, a continual confirmation that his faith in God's forgiveness of himself is a reality. *From Christ* to receive forgiveness, and *like Christ* to bestow it on others: these two are one.

Thus the Scriptures and the Church teach: but, what do the lives and experiences of Christians say? Alas! how many hardly know that thus it is written, or who, if they know it, think it is more than can be expected from a sinful being. How many think that if they agree in general to what has been said, they will always find a reason, in their own particular case, why it should not be so. Others might be strengthened in evil; the offender would never forgive had the injury been done to him. There are very many eminent Christians who do not act so; such excuses are never wanting. And yet, the command is so very simple, and its sanction so very solemn: "Forgive one another, even as God for Christ's sake hath forgiven you" (Ephesians 4:32); "If ye do not forgive, neither will your Father which is in heaven forgive you" (Mark 11:26). With such human reasonings, the Word of God is made of none effect. As though it were not just through forgiving love that God seeks to conquer evil, and therefore forgives even unto seventy times seven. As though it were not plain, that not what the offender would do to me, *but what Christ has done,* must be the rule of my conduct. As though conformity to the example not of Christ Himself, but of pious Christians, were the sign that I have truly received the forgiveness of sins.

Alas! where is there a Church or Christian circle in which the law of forgiving love is not grievously transgressed? How often in our Church assemblies, in philanthropic undertakings, as well as in ordinary social dealings, and even in domestic life, it is evident that to many Christians the call to forgive, just as Christ did, has never yet become a ruling principle of their conduct. Because of a difference of opinion, opposition to a course of action that we considered to be correct, some real or imagined slight, or because of some unkind or thoughtless word, feelings of resentment, contempt, or estrangement have been harbored, instead of loving, forgiving, and forgetting like Christ. In such, the importance of the law of compassion, love, and forgiveness has never yet taken possession of mind and heart. That law, in which the relationship of the head to the members is rooted, must rule the whole relationship of the members to each other.

Beloved followers of Jesus! called to manifest His likeness to the world, learn that as forgiveness of your sins was one of the first things Jesus did for you, forgiveness of others is one of the first that you can do for Him. And remember that to the new heart there is a joy even sweeter than that of being forgiven—the joy of forgiving others. The joy of being forgiven is only that of a sinner and of earth. The joy of forgiving is Christ's own joy, the joy of heaven. Oh, come and see that it is nothing less than the work that Christ Himself does, and the joy with which He Himself is satisfied that you are called to participate in.

It is thus that you can bless the world. It is as the forgiving One that Jesus conquers His enemies, and binds His friends to Himself. It is as the forgiving One that Jesus has set up His Kingdom and continually extends it. It is through the same forgiving love, not only preached but *shown in the life of His disciples,* that the Church will convince the world of God's love. If the world see men and women loving and forgiving as Jesus did, it will be compelled to confess that God is truly with them.

And, if it still appears too hard and too high, remember that this will only be as long as we consult the natural heart. A sinful nature has no taste for this joy, and can never attain it. But, in union with Christ we can do it. He who abides in Him walks even as He walked. If you have surrendered yourself to follow Christ in everything, then He will, by His Holy Spirit, enable you to do this, too. Before you come into temptation, accustom yourself to fixing your gaze on Jesus, in the heavenly beauty of His forgiving love as your example. "Beholding...the glory of the Lord, we are changed into the same image from glory to glory" (2 Corinthians 3:18).

Every time you pray or thank God for forgiveness, make the vow that to the glory of His name you will manifest the same forgiving love to all around you. Before there is a question of forgiveness of others, let your heart be filled with love to Christ, love to the brethren, and love to enemies. A heart full of love finds it blessed to forgive. Let—in each little circumstance of daily life when the temptation not to forgive might arise—the opportunity to show how truly you live in God's forgiving love be joyfully welcomed. Rejoice in how glad you are to let its beautiful light shine through you on others. How blessed a privilege it is to be able to thus bear the image of your beloved Lord.

To forgive like You, blessed Son of God! I take this as the law of my life. You who have given the command, also give the power. You who loved me enough to forgive me, will also fill me with love, and teach me to forgive others. You who gave me the first blessing, in the joy of having my sins forgiven, will surely give me the second blessing, the deeper joy of forgiving others as You have forgiven me. For this reason, fill me with faith in the power of Your love in me, to make me like Yourself, to enable me to forgive the seventy times seven, and so to love and bless all around me.

O my Jesus! Your example is my law. I must be like you. And, Your example is my gospel, too. I can be as You are. What You demand of me by Your example, You work in me by Your life. I will forgive like You.

Lord, only lead me deeper into my dependence on You, into the all-sufficiency of Your grace and the blessed keeping which comes from Your indwelling. Then, I will believe and prove the all-prevailing power of love. I will forgive even as Christ has forgiven me. Amen.

Chapter 20

LIKE CHRIST...
In Beholding Him

"But we all, with open face beholding as in a glass the glory of the Lord, are changed into the same image from glory to glory, even as by the Spirit of the Lord"—2 Corinthians 3:18.

Moses spent forty days on the mount in communion with God. When he came down, his face shown with divine glory. He did not know it himself, but Aaron and the people saw it (see Exodus 34:30). It was so evidently God's glory that Aaron and the people feared to approach him.

In this we have an image of what takes place in the New Testament. The privilege Moses there alone enjoyed is now the portion of every believer. When we behold the glory of God in Christ, in the glass of the Holy Scriptures, His glory shines on us, into us, and fills us until it shines out from us again. By gazing on His glory, the believer is changed through the Spirit into the same image. *Beholding Jesus makes us like Him.*

It is a law of nature that the eye exercises a mighty

influence on mind and character. The education of a child is carried on greatly through the eye. He is molded very much by the manners and habits of those he sees continually. To form and mold our character, the heavenly Father shows us His divine glory in the face of Jesus. He does it in the expectation that it will give us great joy to gaze upon it and because He knows that, by gazing on it, we will be conformed to the same image. Let everyone who desires to be like Jesus note how he can attain to it.

Continually look to the divine glory as seen in Christ. What is the special characteristic of that glory? *It is the manifestation of divine perfection in human form.* The chief marks of the image of the divine glory in Christ are these: His humiliation and His love.

There is the glory of His humiliation. When you see how the eternal Son emptied Himself and became man, and how as man He humbled Himself as a servant and was obedient even unto the death of the cross, you have seen the highest glory of God. The glory of God's omnipotence as Creator, and the glory of God's holiness as King, is not as wonderful as this: the glory of grace which humbled itself as a servant to serve God and man. We must learn to look on this humiliation as true glory. *To be humbled like Christ must be to us the only thing worthy of the name of glory on earth.* It must become, in our eyes, the most beautiful, the most wonderful, the most desirable thing that can be imagined—a very joy to look on or think of. The effect of thus gazing on it and admiring it will be that you will not be able to conceive of any glory greater than to be and act like Jesus. You will long to humble yourself even as He did. Gazing on Jesus, admiring and adoring Him, will work in us the same mind that there was in Him, and so we will be changed into His image.

The glory of His love is inseparable from this. The humiliation leads you back to the love as its origin and power. It is from love that the humiliation gains its beauty. Love is the highest glory of God. But this love was a hidden mystery until it was manifest in Christ Jesus. It is only in His humanity, in His gentle, compassionate, and loving fellowship with men, with foolish, sinful, hostile men, that the glory of divine love was first seen. The soul that gets a glimpse of this glory, and that understands that *to love like Christ is alone worthy of the name of glory,* will long to become like Christ in this. Beholding this glory of the love of God in Christ, he is changed to the same image.

Do you want to be like Christ? Here is the path. Gaze on the glory of God in Him. *In Him,* that is to say, do not look only to the words, the thoughts, and the graces in which His glory is seen, but look to Himself, the living, loving Christ. Behold Him, look into His very eyes. Look into His face, as a loving Friend, as the living God.

Look to Him in adoration. Bow before Him as God. His glory has an almighty, living power to impart itself to us, to pass over into us, and to fill us.

Look to Him in faith. Exercise the blessed trust that He is yours, that He has given Himself to you, and that you have a claim to all that is in Him. It is His purpose to work out His image in you. Behold Him with the joyful and certain expectation: the glory that I behold in Him is destined for me. He will give it to me. As I gaze and wonder and trust, I become like Christ.

Look to Him with a strong desire. Do not yield to the slothfulness of the flesh that is satisfied with less than full conformity to the Lord. Pray God to free you from all carnal contentment with present attainments, and to fill you with the deep, unquenchable longing for His glory. Pray most fervently the prayer of Moses, "Shew me Thy glory" (Exodus 33:18). Let nothing discourage you, not even the apparently slow progress you make. Press onward with ever growing desire after the blessed prospect that God's Word holds out to you: "We are changed into the same image from glory to glory."

And as you behold Him, above all, let the look of love not be wanting. Tell Him continually how He has won your heart, how you do love Him, how entirely you belong to Him. Tell Him that to please Him, the beloved One, is your highest and your only joy. Let the bond of love between you and Him be drawn continually closer. Love unites and makes like.

Like Christ! we can be it, we will be it, each in our own measure. The Holy Spirit is the pledge that it will be. God's Holy Word has said, "We are changed into the same image from glory to glory, even as by *the Spirit of the Lord."* This is the Spirit that was in Jesus, and through whom the divine glory lived and shone on Him. This Spirit is called "The Spirit of glory" (1 Peter 4:14). This Spirit is in us as in the Lord Jesus. It is His work, in our silent, adoring contemplation, to bring over into us and work within us what we see in our Lord Jesus. Through this Spirit, we already have Christ's life in us, with all the gifts of His grace. But, that life must be stirred up and developed. It must grow up, pass into our whole being, take possession of our entire nature, and penetrate and pervade all. We can count on the Spirit to work this in us if we will only yield ourselves to Him and obey Him. As we gaze on Jesus in the Word, He opens our eyes to see the glory of all that Jesus does and is. He makes us willing to be like Him. He strengthens our faith, that what we behold in Jesus can be in us because Jesus Himself is ours. He unceasingly works in us the life of abiding in Christ—a whole-hearted union and communion with Him. He does this according to the promise: "The (Spirit) shall glorify me: for He shall receive of Mine and shall shew it unto you" (John 16:14). We are changed into the image on which we gaze from glory to glory, *as by the Spirit of the Lord.* Let us only understand that the fullness of the Spirit is given to us. He who believingly surrenders himself to be filled with Him will experience how gloriously He accomplishes His work of stamping the image and likeness of Christ on our souls and lives.

Brother! beholding Jesus and His glory, you can confidently expect to become like Him. Only trust yourself in quietness and restfulness of soul to the leading of the Spirit. *"The Spirit of glory and of God resteth upon you"* (1 Peter 4:14). Gaze on and adore the glory of God in Christ; you will be changed with divine power from glory to glory. In the power of the Holy Spirit, the mighty transformation will be worked, your desires will be fulfilled, and *like Christ* will be the blessed, God-given experience of your life.

O my Lord! I do thank You for the glorious assurance that while I am engaged with You, in my work of beholding Your glory, the Holy Spirit is engaged with me, in His work of changing me into that image, and of laying Your glory on me.

Lord! grant me to behold Your glory properly. Moses had been forty days with You when Your glory shone upon Him. I acknowledge that my communion with You has been too short and passing, that I have taken too little time to come under the full impression of what Your image is. Lord! teach me this. Draw me in these my meditations, too, to surrender myself to contemplate and adore until my soul may exclaim: This is glorious! this is the glory of God! O my God, show me Your glory.

And strengthen my faith, blessed Lord! that, even when I am not conscious of any special experience, the Holy Spirit will do His work. Moses did not know that his face shone. Lord! keep me from looking at self. May I be so taken up only with You as to forget and lose myself in You. Lord! it is he who is dead to self who lives in You.

O my Lord, as often as I gaze upon Your image and example, I would do it in the faith that the Holy Spirit will fill me, will take entire possession of me, and so work Your likeness in me that the world may see some of Your glory in me. In this faith, I will venture to take Your precious word, "From glory to glory," as my watchword, to be to me the promise of a grace that grows richer every day, of a blessing that is ever ready to surpass itself, and to make what has been given only the pledge of the better that is to come. Precious Savior! gazing on You, it will indeed be so, "From glory to glory." Amen.

Chapter 21

LIKE CHRIST... In His Humility

"In lowliness of mind let each esteem other better than themselves....Let this mind be in you, which was also in Christ Jesus: Who, being in the form of God...made himself of no reputation, and took upon him the form of a servant, and was made in the likeness of men: and being found in fashion as a man, he humbled himself, became obedient unto death, even the death of the cross"—Philippians 2:3-8.

In this wonderful passage, we have a summary of all the most precious truths that cluster around the person of the blessed Son of God. First, there is His majestic divinity: *"In the form of God," "equal with God."* Then comes the mystery of His incarnation in that word of deep and inexhaustible meaning: *"He made Himself of no reputation."* The atonement follows with the humiliation, obedience, suffering, and death from which it derives its worth: *"He humbled Himself, and became obedient unto death, even the death of the cross."* And all is crowned by

His glorious exhaltation: *"God also hath highly exalted Him"* (Philippians 2:9). Christ as God, Christ becoming man, Christ as man in humiliation working out our redemption, and Christ in glory as Lord of all: such are the treasures of wisdom this passage contains.

Volumes have been written on the discussion of some of the words the passage contains. And yet, sufficient attention has not always been given to the connection in which the Holy Spirit gives this wondrous teaching. It's primary importance is not as a statement of truth for the refutation of error, or the strengthening of faith. The object is a very different one. There was still pride and a lack of love among the Philippians. It is with the distinct view of setting Christ's example before them, and teaching them to humble themselves as He did, that this portion of inspiration was given: "In lowliness of mind let each esteem other better than themselves....Let this mind be in you, which was also in Christ Jesus." He who does not study this portion of God's Word with the wish to become lowly as Christ was, has never used it for the one great purpose for which God gave it. Christ descending from the throne of God, and seeking His way back there as man through the humiliation of the cross, reveals the only way by which we can ever reach that throne. The faith which, with His atonement, also accepts His example is alone true faith. Each soul that truly wants to belong to Him must have His Spirit, His disposition, and His image in union with Him.

"Let this mind be in you, which was also in Christ Jesus: Who being in the form of God....made Himself of no reputation and...as a man humbled Himself." We must be like Christ in His self-emptying and self-humiliation. The first great act of self-denial, in which as God He emptied Himself of His divine glory and power and laid it aside, was followed by the no less wondrous humbling of Himself as man—the death of the cross. And in this amazing, twofold humiliation, the astonishment of the universe, and the delight of the Father, Holy Scripture very simply says that we must, as a matter of course, be like Christ.

And do Paul, the Scriptures, and God really expect this of us? Why not? Or rather, how can they expect anything else? Indeed, they know the fearful power of pride and the old Adam in our nature. But, they know also that Christ has redeemed us not only from the curse but from the power of sin, and that He gives us His resurrection life and power to enable us to live as He did on earth. They say that He is not only our Surety, but our Example as well. We not only live through Him, but like Him. And further, not only is He our Example, but also our Head, who lives in us, and continues in us the life He once led on earth. With such a Christ, and such a plan of redemption, can it be otherwise? The follower of Christ must have the same mind as was in Christ. He must especially be like Him in His humility.

Christ's example teaches us that it is not sin that must humble us. This is what many Christians think.

They consider daily falls to be necessary in order to remain humble. This is not so. There is indeed a humility that is very lovely, and of such great value as the beginning of something more, which consists in the acknowledgement of transgression and shortcomings. But, there is a humility which is more heavenly still, and which consists, even when grace keeps us from sinning, in the self-abasement that can only wonder that God should bless us. It delights to be as nothing before Him to whom we owe all. It is grace we need, and not sin, to make and keep us humble. The heaviest laden branches always bow the lowest. The greatest flow of water makes the deepest river bed. The nearer the soul comes to God, the more His majestic presence makes it feel its littleness. It is this alone that makes it possible for each to esteem others better than himself. Jesus Christ, the Holy One of God, is our example of humility. It was because He knew that the Father had given all things into His hands, and that He was come from God and went to God, that He washed the disciples' feet. It is the divine presence, the consciousness of the divine life and the divine love in us, that will make us humble.

To many Christians, it appears impossible to say: I will not think of self; I will esteem others better than myself. They ask grace to overcome the worst outbursts of pride and vainglory, but an entire self-renunciation, such as Christ's, is too difficult and too high for them. If they only understood the deep truth and blessedness of the word, "He that humbleth himself shall be exalted" (Luke 14:11), "He who loses his life for My sake shall find it" (Matthew 16:25), they would not be satisfied with anything less than entire conformity to their Lord in this. And, they would find that there is a way to overcome self and self-exhaltation. There is a way to see it nailed to Christ's cross, and there keep it crucified continually through the Spirit (see Galatians 5:24; Romans 8:13). Only he who heartily yields himself to live in the fellowship of Christ's death can grow to such humility.

To attain this, two things are necessary. The first is a fixed purpose and surrender to be nothing and seek nothing for oneself, but to live only for God and our neighbor. The other is the faith which appropriates the power of Christ's death as being our death to sin and our deliverance from its power. This fellowship of Christ's death brings an end to the life in which sin is *too strong for us.* It is the commencement of a life in us in which *Christ is too strong for sin.*

It is only under the teaching and powerful working of the Holy Spirit that one can realize, accept, and keep hold of this truth. But God be thanked, we have the Holy Spirit. Oh, that we may fully trust ourselves to His guidance. He *will* guide us; it is His work. He will glorify Christ in us. He will teach us to understand that we are dead to sin and the old self, that Christ's life and humility are ours.

Thus Christ's humility is appropriated in faith. This may take place at once. But, the appropriation in experience is gradual. Our thoughts and feelings, our very manners and conversation, have been so long under the dominion of the old self, that it takes time to saturate and permeate and transfigure them with the heavenly light of Christ's humility. At first, the conscience is not perfectly enlightened, the spiritual taste and the power of discernment have not yet been exercised. But with each believing renewal of the consecration in the depth of the soul: "I have surrendered myself to be humble like Jesus," power will go out from Him. It will fill the whole being, until in face, voice, and action the sanctification of the Spirit will be observable, and the Christian will truly be clothed with humility.

The blessedness of a Christlike humility is unspeakable. It is of great worth in the sight of God: "He giveth grace unto the humble" (James 4:6). In the spiritual life, it is the source of rest and joy. To the humble all God does is right and good. Humility is always ready to praise God for the least of His mercies. Humility does not find it difficult to trust. It submits unconditionally to all that God says. The two people in the Bible whom Jesus praises for their great faith are those who thought least of themselves. The centurion had said, "I am not worthy that Thou shouldest come under my roof" (Matthew 8:8); the Syrophoenician woman was content to be numbered with the dogs. In fellowship with men, it is the secret of blessing and love. The humble man does not take offense, and is very careful not to give it. He is always ready to serve his neighbor, because he has learned from Jesus the divine beauty of being a servant. He finds favor with God and man.

Oh, what a glorious calling for the followers of Christ! To be sent into the world by God to prove that there is nothing more divine than self-humiliation. The humble glorifies God, leads others to glorify Him, and he will at last be glorified with Him. Who would not want to be humble like Jesus?

O Lord, You descended from heaven, and humbled Yourself to the death of the cross. You call me to take Your humility as the law of my life.

Lord, teach me to understand the absolute need of this. A proud follower of the humble Jesus this I cannot, I may not, be. In the secrecy of my heart, my closet, in my house, in the presence of friends or enemies, and in prosperity or adversity, I want to be filled with Your humility.

O my beloved Lord! I feel the need of a new, a deeper insight into Your crucifixion, and my part in it. Reveal to me how my old proud self is crucified with You. Show me in the light of Your Spirit how I, God's regenerate child, am dead to sin and its power, and how, in communion with You, sin is powerless. Lord Jesus, who has conquered sin, strengthen in me the faith that You are my life, and that You will fill me with Your humility if I will submit to be filled with Yourself and the Holy Spirit.

Lord, my hope is in You. In faith in You, I go into the world to show how the same mind that was in You is also in Your children, and teaches us in lowliness of mind each to esteem others better than himself. May God help us. Amen.

Chapter 22

LIKE CHRIST...
In The Likeness Of His Death

"For if we have been planted together in the likeness of his death, we shall be also in the likeness of his resurrection....For in that he died, he died unto sin once....Likewise reckon ye also yourselves to be dead unto sin, but alive unto God through Jesus Christ our Lord"—Romans 6:5,10,11.

We owe our salvation to the death of Christ. The better we understand the meaning of that death, the richer our experience of its power will be. In these words, we are taught what it is to be one with Christ in the likeness of His death. Let everyone who truly longs to be like Christ in his life, seek to correctly know what the likeness of His death means.

Christ had a double work to accomplish in His death. The one was to work out righteousness for us. The other was to obtain life for us. When Scripture speaks of the first part of this work, it uses the expression, *Christ died for our sins.* He took sin upon Himself—bore its punishment. Thus, He made atonement, and brought us a righteousness in which we could stand before God.

When Scripture speaks of the second part of this work, it uses the expression, *He died to sin. Dying for sin* refers to the judicial relationship between Him and sin. God laid our sin upon Him, and through His death, atonement is made for sin before God. *Dying to sin* also refers to a personal relationship through His death, the connection in which He stood to sin was entirely dissolved. During His life, sin had great power to cause Him conflict and suffering: His death ended all of this. Sin no longer had power to tempt or to hurt Him. He was beyond its reach. Death had completely separated Him and sin. Christ died to sin.

Like Christ, the believer has also died to sin—he is one with Him in the likeness of His death. And, as the knowledge that Christ died for sin as our atonement is indispensable to our *justification*, so the knowledge that Christ—and we with Him in the likeness of His death—is dead to sin is indispensable to our *sanctification*. Let us endeavor to understand this.

It was as the second Adam that Christ died. With the first Adam, we had been planted together in the likeness of *his* death. He died, and we with him, and the power of his death works in us. We have in very deed died in him, as truly as he himself died. We understand this. Likewise, we are one plant with Christ in the likeness of His death: He died to sin, and we in Him. And now, the power of His death works in us. We are indeed dead to sin, as truly so as

He Himself is.

Through our first birth, we were made partakers in Adam's death. Through our second birth, we became partakers in the death of the second Adam. Every believer who accepts Christ is partaker of the power of His death, and is dead to sin. But, a believer may be ignorant of much of what he has. In their conversion, most believers are so occupied with Christ's death *for sin* as their justification, that they do not seek to know what it means that in Him they are dead *to sin*. When they first learn to feel their need of Him as their sanctification, then the desire is awakened to understand this likeness of His death. They find the secret of holiness in it—that as Christ, so they also have died to sin.

The Christian who does not understand this always imagines that sin is too strong for Him, that sin still has power over him, and that he must sometimes obey it. But, he thinks this because he does not know that he, like Christ, is dead to sin. If He only believed and understood what this means, his language would be, "Christ has died to sin. Sin has nothing more to say to Him. In His life and death sin had power over Him. It was sin that caused Him the sufferings of the cross, and the humiliation of the grave. But He is dead to sin. It has lost all claim over Him, and He is entirely and forever freed from its power. Even so I as a believer. The new life that is in me is the life of Christ from the dead, a life that has been begotten through death, *a life that is entirely dead to sin.*" The believer, as a new creature in

Christ Jesus, can glory and say: "Like Christ, I am dead to sin. Sin has no right or power over me whatever. I am freed from it, therefore, I need not sin."

And, if the believer still sins, it is because he does not use his privilege to live as one who is dead to sin. Through ignorance, unwatchfulness, or unbelief, he forgets the meaning and the power of this likeness of Christ's death, and sins. But, if he firmly believes in what his participation with Christ's death signifies, he has the power to overcome sin. He truly understands that it is not said, "Sin is dead." No, sin is not dead. Sin still lives and works in the flesh. But, he himself is dead to sin, and alive to God. And so, sin cannot for a single moment, without his consent, have dominion over him. If he sins, it is because he allows it to reign, and submits himself to obey it.

Beloved Christian, who seeks to be like Christ, take the likeness of His death as one of the most glorious parts of the life you want to lead. First of all, appropriate it in faith. Believe that you are indeed dead to sin. Let it be a settled thing. God says it to every one of His children, even the weakest. Say it before Him, too, "Like Christ, I am dead to sin." Do not be afraid to say it; it is the truth. Ask the Holy Spirit to earnestly enlighten you with regard to this part of your union with Christ, so that it may not only be a doctrine, but power and truth.

Endeavor to more deeply understand what it means to live as dead to sin, as one who, in dying, has been freed from its dominion, and who can now reign in life through Jesus Christ over it. Then, the conformity to His death will follow the likeness of His death. It will be gradually and increasingly appropriated as Christ's death manifests its full power in all the faculties and powers of your life. (See Philippians 3.)

And in order to have the full benefit of this likeness of Christ's death, notice two things in particular. The one is the obligation under which it brings you, "How can we who are dead to sin live in it any longer?" Endeavor to enter more deeply into the meaning of this death of Christ into which you have been baptized. His death meant: Rather die than sin—willing to die in order to overcome sin—dead, and therefore released from the power of sin. Let this your be position as well: "Know ye not, that so many of us as were baptized into Jesus Christ were baptized into His death?" (Romans 6:3). Let the Holy Spirit baptize you continually deeper into His death, until the power of God's Word—dead to sin until the conformity to Christ's death—is discernible in all your walk and conversation.

The other lesson is this: The likeness of Christ's death is not only an obligation, but a power. O Christian longing to be Christlike, if there is one thing you need more than and above all else, it is this: know the exceeding greatness of God's power which works in you. It was in the power of eternity that Christ, in His death, wrestled with the powers of hell and conquered them. You have part with Christ in His death; you have part in all the powers by which He conquered. Yield yourself joyfully and believingly to be led more deeply into the conformity to Christ's death. Then, you can do nothing other than become like Him.

O my Lord! how little I have understood Your grace. I have often read the words, "planted into the likeness of His death," and seen that as You died to sin, so it is said to Your believing people, "Likewise also ye." But I have not understood its power. And so, not knowing the likeness of Your death, I did not know that I was free from the power of sin, and as a conqueror could have dominion over it. Lord, You have indeed opened to me a glorious prospect. The man who believingly accepts the likeness of Your death, and according to Your Word considers himself dead to sin, will not be dominated by sin. He has power to live for God.

Lord, let the Holy Spirit reveal this to me more perfectly. I wish to take Your Word in simple faith, and to take the position You assign me as one who in You is dead to sin. Lord, *in You* I am dead to sin. Teach me to hold it fast, or rather to hold You fast in faith, until my whole life is a proof of it. O Lord, take me up and keep me in communion with Yourself, that, abiding in You, I may find *in You* the death unto sin and the life unto God. Amen.

Chapter 23

LIKE CHRIST...
In The Likeness Of His Resurrection

"For if we have been planted together in the likeness of his death, we shall be also in the likeness of his resurrection...that like as Christ was raised up from the dead by the glory of the Father, even so we also should walk in newness of life"—Romans 6:5,4.

Of necessity, the likeness of His death is followed by the likeness of His resurrection. To speak alone of the likeness of His death—of bearing the cross, and of self-denial—gives a one-sided view of following Christ. It is only the power of His resurrection that gives us strength to go on from that likeness of His death, which we at once receive by faith, to that conformity to His death, which comes as the growth of the inner life. Being dead with Christ refers more to the death of the old life to sin and the world which we abandon. Risen with Christ refers to the new life through which the Holy Spirit expels the old. To the Christian who earnestly desires to walk as Christ did, the knowledge of this likeness of His resurrection is indispensable. Let us see if we do not here get the answer to the question as to where we must find strength to live in the world as Christ did.

We have already seen how our Lord's life, before His death, was a life of weakness. As our Surety, sin had great power over Him. It also had power over His disciples, so that He could not give them the Holy Spirit, or do for them what He wished. But, with the resurrection, all was changed. Raised by the almighty power of God, His resurrection life was full of the power of eternity. He had not only conquered death and sin for Himself, but for His disciples also, so that He could, from the first day, make them partakers of His Spirit, His joy, and His heavenly power.

When the Lord Jesus now makes us partakers of His life, it is not the life that He had before His death, but the resurrection life that He won through death. This new life is a life in which sin is already ended and put away, a life that has already conquered hell, the devil, the world, and the flesh, and a life of divine power in human nature. This is the life that likeness to His resurrection gives us: "In that He liveth, He liveth unto God. Likewise reckon ye also yourselves...alive unto God through Jesus Christ our Lord" (Romans 6:10-11). Oh, that through the Holy Spirit God might reveal to us the glory of the life in the likeness of Christ's resurrection! In it, we find the secret of power for a life of conformity to Him.

To most Christians this is a mystery, and therefore their life is full of sin and weakness and defeat. They believe in Christ's resurrection as the sufficient proof of their justification. They think that He had to rise again to continue His work in heaven as Mediator. But, they have no idea that He rose again, so that His glorious resurrection life might now be *the very power of their daily life.* Hence, their hopelessness when they hear of following Jesus fully, and being perfectly conformed to His image. They cannot imagine how a sinner can be required to act as Christ would have acted in all things. They do not know Christ in the power of His resurrection, or the mighty power with which His life now works in those who are willing to count all things but loss for His sake (see Philippians 3:8; Ephesians 1:19-20). Come, all you who are weary of a life unlike Jesus, and long to walk always in His footsteps. You will begin to see that there is, in the Scriptures, a better life for you than you have thus far known. Come and let me try to show you the unspeakable treasure that is yours in your likeness to Christ in His resurrection. Let me ask three questions.

The first is: Are you ready to surrender your life to the rule of Jesus and His resurrection life? I do not doubt that the contemplation of Christ's example has convinced you of sin in more than one point. In seeking your own will and glory instead of God's, in ambition, pride, selfishness, and want of love toward man, you have seen how far you are from the obedience, humility, and love of Jesus. And now it is the question of whether or not, in view of all these things in which you have acknowledged as sin, you are willing to say: If Jesus will take possession of my life, then I resign all right or wish ever to have the least to do with my own will. I give my life, with all I have and am entirely to Him, always to do what He through His Word and Spirit commands me. If He will *live and rule in me,* I promise unbounded and hearty obedience.

Faith is needed for such a surrender. Therefore, the second question is: Are you prepared to believe that Jesus will take possession of the life entrusted to Him, and that He will rule and keep it? When the believer intrusts his entire spiritual and temporal life completely to Christ, then he learns to correctly understand Paul's words: "I am dead; I live no more: Christ liveth in me" (see Galatians 2:20). Dead with Christ and risen again, the living Christ in His resurrection life takes possession of and rules my new life. The resurrection life is not a thing that I may have if I can undertake to keep it. No, this is just what I cannot do. But blessed be God! *Jesus Christ Himself is the resurrection and the life*—is the resurrection life. *He Himself will, from day to day and hour to hour, see to it and insure that I live as one who is risen with Him.* He does it through that Holy Spirit who is the Spirit of His risen life. The Holy Spirit is in us, and will, if we trust Jesus for it, continually maintain the presence and power of the risen Lord within us. We need not fear that we never can succeed in leading such a holy life as becomes those who are temples of the living God. *We are indeed not able.* But, it is not required of us. The living Jesus, who is the resurrection, has shown His power over all our enemies. He Himself, who so loves us, will work it in us. He gives us the Holy Spirit as our power, and He will perform His work in us with divine faithfulness if we will only trust Him. *Christ Himself is our life.*

And now comes the third question: Are you ready to use this resurrection life for the purpose for which God gave it to Him, and gives it to you, as a power of blessing to the lost? All desires after the resurrection life will fail if we are only seeking our own perfection and happiness. God raised up and exalted Jesus to give repentance and remission of sins. He always lives to pray for sinners. Yield yourself to receive His resurrection life with the same aim. Give yourself wholly to working and praying for the perishing. Then, you will become a fit vessel and instrument in which the resurrection life can dwell and work out its glorious purposes.

Brethren! your calling is to live like Christ. To this end *you have already been made one with Him* in the likeness of His resurrection. The only question is now whether or not you desire the full experience of His resurrection life, whether or not you are willing to surrender your whole life so that He may manifest resurrection power in every part of it. I beg you, do not draw back. Offer yourself unreservedly to Him, with all your weakness and unfaithfulness. Believe that as His resurrection was a wonder above all thought and expectation, so He as the Risen One will still work in you exceeding abundantly above all you could think or desire.

What a difference there was in the life of the disciples before Jesus' death and after His resurrection! Before, all was weakness and fear, self and sin. With the resurrection, all was power and joy, life and love and glory.

The change will be just as great when a believer—who has known Jesus' resurrection only as the ground of his justification, but has not known of the *likeness* of His resurrection—discovers how the Risen One will Himself be his life. How wonderful it will be when he realizes that Jesus Himself will take on the responsibility for the whole of his life. Oh, brethren, who have not yet experienced this, who are troubled and weary because you are called to walk like Christ and cannot do it, come and taste the blessedness of giving your whole life to the Risen Savior in the assurance that He will live it for you.

O Lord! my soul adores You as the Prince of life! On the cross, You conquered each one of my enemies—the devil, the flesh, the world, and sin. As Conqueror, You rose to manifest and maintain the power of Your risen life in Your people. You made them one with Yourself in the likeness of Your resurrection. Now, You will live in them, and show forth in their earthly life the power of Your heavenly life.

Praised be Your name for this wonderful grace. Blessed Lord, I come at Your invitation to offer and surrender my life and all it implies, to You. Too long have I striven in my own strength to live like You, and not succeeded. The more I sought to walk like You, the deeper was my disappointment. I have heard of Your disciples who tell how blessed it is to cast all care and responsibility for their life on You. Lord, I am risen with You, one with You in the likeness of Your resurrection. Come and take me entirely for Your own, and be my life.

Above all, I beseech You, O my Risen Lord, reveal Yourself to me, as You did to Your first disciples in the power of Your resurrection. It was not enough that after Your resurrection You appeared to Your disciples. They did not know You until *You made Yourself known.* Lord Jesus! I do believe in *You. Be pleased to make Yourself known to me as my life.* It is Your work; You alone can do it. I trust You for it. And so, my resurrection life will be like Your own—a continual source of light and blessing to all who are needing You. Amen.

Chapter 24

LIKE CHRIST...
Being Made Conformable To His Death

"That I may know him, and the power of his resurrection, and the fellowship of his sufferings, being made conformable unto his death"—Philippians 3:10.

We know that the death of Christ was the death of the cross. We know that that death of the cross is His chief glory. Without that death He would not be the Christ. The distinguishing characteristic, the one mark by which He is separated here in earth and in heaven from all other persons—both in the divine Being and in God's universe—is this one: He is the Crucified Son of God. Of all the characteristics of conformity, this must necessarily be the chief and most glorious one—conformity to His death.

This is what made it so attractive to Paul. What had been Christ's glory and blessedness must have been his glory, too. He knew that the most intimate likeness to Christ is conformity to His death. What that death had been to Christ it would be to him, as he grew conformed to it.

Christ's death on the cross had been the end of sin. During His life it could tempt Him. When He died on the cross, He died to sin—it could no longer reach Him. Conformity to Christ's death is the power to keep us from the power of sin. As I, by the grace of the Holy Spirit, am kept in my position as crucified with Christ, and live out my crucifixion life as the Crucified One lives it in me, I am kept from sinning.

Christ's death on the cross was a sweet-smelling sacrifice, infinitely pleasing to the Father. Oh, if I want to dwell in the favor and love of the Father, and be His delight, I am sure there is nothing which gives such deep and perfect access to it as being conformable to Christ's death. To the Father, there is nothing in the universe so beautiful, so holy, so heavenly, so wonderful as this sight—the Crucified Jesus. And, the closer I can get to Him, and the more conformed to His death I can become, the more surely I will enter into the very bosom of His love.

Christ's death on the cross was the entrance to the power of the resurrection life, the unchanging life of eternity. In our spiritual life, we often have to mourn the breaks, failures, and intervals which prove to us that there is still something wanting that prevents the resurrection life from asserting its full power. The secret is here: there is still some subtle, self-life which has not yet been brought into the perfect conformity of Christ's death. We can be sure that nothing is needed except a fuller entrance into the fellowship of the cross to make us the full partakers of the resurrection joy.

Above all, it was Christ's death on the cross that made Him the life of the world, gave Him the power to bless and to save (see John 12:24-25). In the conformity to Christ's death, there is an end of self. We give up ourselves to live and die for others. We are full of the faith that our surrender of ourselves to bear the sin of others is accepted by the Father. Out of this death, we rise with the power to love and to bless.

And now, what is this conformity to the death of the cross that brings such blessings, and in what does it consist? We see it in Jesus. The cross means entire self-denial. The cross means the death of self—the utter surrender of our own will and our life to be lost in the will of God, to let God's will do with us what it pleases. This was what the cross meant to Jesus. It cost Him a terrible struggle before He could give Himself up to it. When He was sore amazed, very heavy, and His soul exceedingly sorrowful unto death, it was because His whole being shrank back from that cross and its curse. Three times He had to pray before He could fully say, "Not my will, but Thine, be done" (Luke 22:42). But He did say it. And His giving Himself up to the cross is to say: Let me do anything, rather than that God's will should not be done. I give up everything—only God's will must be done.

And, being made conformable to Christ's death is that we so give away ourselves and our whole life—with its power of willing and acting—to God, that we learn to be, work, and do nothing but what God reveals to us as His will. And, such a life is called conformity to the death of Christ. It is so, not only because it is somewhat similar to His, but because it is Himself by His Holy Spirit just repeating and acting over again in us the life that animated Him in His crucifixion. Were it not for this, the very thought of such conformity would be like blasphemy.

But now it is not so. In the power of the Holy Spirit, as the Spirit of the Crucified Jesus, the believer knows that the blessed resurrection life has its power and its glory from its being a crucifixion life, begotten from the cross. He yields himself to it; he believes that it has possession of him. Realizing that he himself does not have the power to think or do anything that is good or holy—that the power of the flesh asserts itself and defiles everything that is in him—he yields and holds every power of his being, as far as his disposal of them goes, in the place of crucifixion and condemnation. And so, he yields and holds every power of his being, every faculty of body, soul, and spirit, at the disposal of Jesus. The distrust and denial of self in everything, the trust of Jesus in everything, mark his life. The very spirit of the cross breathes through his whole being.

And, it is so far from being, as it might appear, a matter of painful strain and weary effort to thus maintain the crucifixion position. To one who knows Christ in the power of His resurrection—for Paul puts this first—and so is made conformed to His death, it is rest and strength and victory. It is not the dead cross—not self's self-denial, not a work in his own strength—that he has to do with, but the living Jesus, in whom the crucifixion is an accomplished thing—already passed into the life of resurrection. "I am crucified with Christ....Christ liveth in me" (Galatians 2:20). It is this that gives the courage and the desire for an every growing, ever deeper entrance into most perfect conformity with His death.

And how is this blessed conformity to be attained? Paul will give us the answer. "*What things were gain to me,* those I counted loss for Christ. Yea, doubtless, and I count *all things* but loss for the excellency of the knowledge of Jesus Christ my Lord...that I may know Him...being made conformable unto His death" (Philippians 3:7-10). The pearl is of great price, but oh! it is worth the purchase. Let us give up all, yes all, to be admitted by Jesus to a place with Him on the cross.

And, if it appears hard to give up all, and then have our only reward be a whole lifetime on the cross, oh, let us listen again to Paul as he tells us what made him so willingly give up all, and so intently choose the cross. It was Jesus—Christ Jesus, my Lord. The cross was the place where he could get into fullest union with his Lord. To know *Him*, to win *Him,* to be found in *Him*, to be made *like to Him*—this was the burning passion that made it easy to cast away all, and that gave the cross such mighty, attractive power. Anything to come nearer to Jesus. All for Jesus, was his motto. It contains the twofold answer to the question, How to attain this conformity to Christ's death? The one is, Cast out all. The other, And let Jesus come in. *All for Jesus.*

Yes, it is only knowing Jesus that can make the conformity to His death at all possible. But, let the soul win *Him*, be found in *Him*, and know *Him* in the power of the resurrection, and it becomes more than possible—a blessed reality. Therefore, beloved follower of Jesus, look to Him, look to Him, the Crucified One. Gaze on Him until your soul has learned to say: O my Lord, I must be like You. Gaze until you have seen how He Himself, the Crucified One, in His ever-present omnipotence, draws near to live in you and breathe through your being His crucifixion life. It was through the eternal Spirit that He offered Himself unto God. That Spirit brings and imparts all that that death on the cross is, means, and effected to you as your life. By that Holy Spirit, Jesus Himself maintains in each soul who can trust Him for it, the power of the cross as an abiding death to sin and self. It is a never ceasing source of resurrection life and power. Therefore, once again, look to Him, the Living, Crucified Jesus.

But remember, above all, that while you have to seek the best and the highest with all your might, the full blessing does not come as the fruit of your efforts, but unsought—a free gift to whom it is given from above. It is as it pleases the Lord Jesus to reveal Himself that we are made conformable to His death. Therefore, seek and get it *from Him.*

O Lord, such knowledge is too wonderful for me.

It is too high, and I cannot attain to it. To know You in the power of Your resurrection, and to be made conformable to Your death: these are the things which are hid from the wise and prudent, and are revealed unto babes—unto those elect souls alone, to whom it is given to know the mysteries of the Kingdom.

O my Lord! I see more than ever utter folly it is to think of likeness to You as an attainment through my effort. I cast myself on Your mercy. Look upon me according to the greatness of Your loving-kindness, and of Your free favor, reveal Yourself to me. If You will be pleased to come forth from Your heavenly dwelling place to draw close to me, to prepare me, and to take me up into the full fellowship of Your life and death, O my Lord, then I will live and die for You, and the souls You have died to save.

Blessed Savior! I know You are willing. Your love to each of Your redeemed ones is infinite. O teach me; draw me to give up all for You, and take eternal possession of me for Yourself. And oh! let some measure of conformity to Your death, in its self-sacrifice for the perishing, be the mark of my life. Amen.

Chapter 25

LIKE CHRIST . . .
Giving His Life For Men

"Whosoever will be great among you, let him be your minister; and whosoever will be chief among you, let him be your servant; even as the Son of man came not to be ministered unto, but to minister, and to give his life a ransom for many"—Matthew 20:26-28.

"Hereby perceive we the love of God, because he laid down his life for us: and we ought to lay down our lives for the brethren"—1 John 3:16.

In speaking of the likeness of Christ's death, and of being made conformable to it—of bearing the cross and being crucified with Him—there is one danger to which even the earnest believer is exposed. That danger is seeking after these blessings for his own sake, or, as he thinks, for the glory of God in his own personal perfection. The error would be a fatal one. He would never attain the close conformity to Jesus' death he hoped for. He would be leaving out that which is the essential element in the death of Jesus, and in the self-sacrifice it instills. That characteristic is its absolute unselfishness, its reference to others. To be made conformable to Christ's death implies a dying to self, a losing sight of self altogether in giving up and laying down our life for others. To the question, how far we are to go in living for, loving, serving, and saving men, the Scriptures do not hesitate to give the unequivocal answer: We are to go as far as Jesus, even to the laying down of our life. We are to consider this the entire object for which we are redeemed, and are left in the world. The one object for which we live is the laying down of life in death which follows as a matter of course. Like Christ, the only thing that keeps us in this world is to be the glory of God in the salvation of sinners. Scripture does not hesitate to say that it is in His path of suffering, as He goes to work out atonement and redemption, that we are to follow Him.

How clearly this comes out in the words of the Master Himself: "Whosoever will be chief among you, let him be your servant, even as the Son of man came not to be ministered unto, but to minister, and to give His life a ransom for many." The highest in glory will be he who was lowest in service, and most like the Master in His giving His life a ransom. And so again, a few days later, He spoke of His own death in the words: "The hour is come, that the Son of man should be glorified. Verily, verily, I say unto you, Except a corn of wheat fall into the ground and die, it abideth alone: but if it die, it bringeth forth much fruit" (John 12:23-24). He emphasized, to His disciples, what He had said by repeating what they had already heard spoken, "He that loveth his life shall lose it; and he that hateth his life in this world shall keep it unto life eternal" (John 12:25). The corn of wheat dying to rise again, losing its life to regain it multiplied manifold, is clearly set forth as the emblem not only of the Master but of each of His followers. Loving life, refusing to die, means remaining alone in selfishness. Losing life to bring forth much fruit in others is the only way to keep it for ourselves. There is no way to find our life but as Jesus did—in giving it up for the salvation of others. Herein is the Father, herein shall we be glorified. The deepest underlying thought of conformity to Christ's death is giving our life to God for saving others. Without this, the longing for conformity to that death is in danger of being a refined selfishness.

How remarkably the Apostle Paul exhibits this spirit, and how instructive are the words which the Holy Spirit expressed in him. To the Corinthians he says: "Always bearing about in the body the dying of the Lord Jesus, that the life also of Jesus might be made manifest in our body. For we which live are always delivered unto death for Jesus' sake, that the life also of Jesus might be made manifest in our mortal flesh. So then *death worketh in us, but life in you"* (2 Corinthians 4:10-12). "Though *He was crucified through weakness,* yet He liveth by the power of God. For *we also are weak in Him,* but we shall live with Him by the power of God toward you" (2 Corinthians 13:4). "I now rejoice *in my sufferings for you,* and fill up that which is behind of the afflictions of Christ in my flesh for His body's sake, which is the church" (Colossians 1:24). These passages teach us how the vicarious element of the suffering that Christ bore in His body on the tree, to a certain extent, still characterizes the suffering of His body the Church.

Believers who give themselves up to bear the burden of the sins of men before the Lord, who suffer reproach, shame, weariness, and pain, in the effort to win souls, are filling up the afflictions of Christ, which they lack, in their flesh. The power and the fellowship of His suffering and death work the power of Christ's life through them in those for whom they labor in love. There is no doubt that in the fellowship of His sufferings, and the conformity to His death in Philippians 3, Paul had the inner spiritual involvement in mind, as well as the external bodily participation in the suffering of Christ.

And so it must be with each of us in some measure. Self-sacrifice, not merely for the sake of our own sanctification, but for the salvation of our fellow-men, is what brings us into true fellowship with the Christ who gave Himself for us.

The practical application of these thoughts is very simple. Let us first of all try to *see* the truth the Holy Spirit seeks to teach us. As the most essential thing in likeness to Christ is likeness to His death, so the most essential thing in likeness to His death is the giving up of our life to win others to God. It is a death in which all thought of saving self is lost in that of saving others. Let us pray for the light of the Holy

Spirit to show us this. We must learn to feel that we are in the world just as Christ was, to give up self, to love and serve, to live and die, "even as the Son of man came not to be ministered unto, but to minister, and to give His life a ransom for many." Oh, that God would allow His people to know their calling—they do not belong to themselves, but to God *and to their fellow-men.* Even as Christ, they are only to live to be a blessing to the world.

Then, let us *believe* in the grace that is waiting to make our experience of this truth a reality. Let us believe that God accepts our giving up of our whole life for His glory in the saving of others. Let us believe that conformity to the death of Jesus in this, its very life principle, is what the Holy Spirit will work out in us. Let us above all believe in Jesus. It is He Himself who will take up every soul that, in full surrender, yields itself to Him and the full fellowship of His death—of His dying in love to bring forth much fruit. Yes, let us believe, and believing seek from above, as the work and the gift of Jesus, likeness to Jesus in this, too.

And, let us at once begin to *act* this faith. Let us put it into practice. Looking upon ourselves now as wholly given up, just like Christ, to live and die for God in our fellow-men, let us with new zeal exercise the ministry of love in winning souls. As we wait for Christ to work out His likeness, as we trust the Holy Spirit to give His mind in us more perfectly, let us in faith begin to act as followers of Him who only lived and died to be a blessing to others. Let our love open the way to the work it has to do by the kindness, gentleness, and helpfulness with which it shines out on all whom we meet in daily life. Let it give itself to the work of intercession, and look up to God to use us as one of His instruments in the answering of those prayers. Let us speak and work for Jesus as those who have a mission and a power from on high which make us sure of a blessing. Let us make soul-winning our object. Let us band ourselves with the great army of reapers the Lord is sending out into His harvest. And before we know of it, we will find that giving our life to win others for God is the most blessed way of dying to self, of being even as the Son of man was—a servant and a Savior of the lost.

O most wonderful and inconceivably blessed likeness to Christ! He gave Himself to men, but could not really reach them, until He gave Himself *a sacrifice to God* for them—the seed corn died, the life was poured out. Then, the blessing flowed forth in mighty power. I may seek to love and serve men. I can only really influence and bless them as I yield myself *unto God* and give up my life into His hands for them. As I lose myself as an offering on the altar, I indeed become, in His spirit and power, a blessing. With my spirit given into His hands, He can use and bless me.

O most blessed God! Do You ask me to come and give myself, my very life, wholly, even unto death, to You for my fellow-men? If I have heard the words of the Master correctly, You do, indeed, seek nothing less.

O God! will You indeed have me? Will You, in Christ, permit me, like Him, as a member of His body, to live and die for those around me? to lay myself, I say it in deep reverence, beside Him on the altar of death, crucified with Him, and be a living sacrifice to You for men? Lord! I do praise You for this most wonderful grace. And now I come, Lord God! and give myself. Oh, for the grace of the Holy Spirit to make the transaction definite and real! Lord! here I am, given up to You, to live only for those whom You are seeking to save.

Blessed Jesus! come and breathe Your own mind and love within me. Take possession of me, my thoughts to think, my heart to feel, my powers to work, my life to live, as given away to God for men. Write it in my heart. It is done; I am given away to God; He has taken me. Keep me each day as in His hands, expecting and assured that He will use me. The life in power, and the outbreaking of the blessing in fullness and power followed Your giving up of Yourself. It will be so in Your people, too. Glory to Your name. Amen.

Chapter 26

LIKE CHRIST...
In His Meekness

"Behold, thy King cometh unto thee, meek"—Matthew 21:5.

"Learn of me, for I am meek and lowly in heart: and ye shall find rest unto your souls"—Matthew 11:29.

The first of these two words is written about our Lord Jesus on His way to the cross. It is in His sufferings that the meekness of Jesus is especially manifested. Follower of Jesus—so ready to take your place under the shadow of His cross, and there to behold the Lamb slain for your sins—is it not a precious thought that there is one part of His work, as the suffering Lamb of God, in which you may bear His image and be like Him every day? You can be meek and gentle even as He was.

Meekness is the opposite of all that is hard or bitter or sharp. It refers to the disposition which makes us compassionate toward our inferiors. "With meekness," ministers must instruct those who oppose them, and who teach and bring back the erring (see Galatians 6:1; 2 Timothy 2:25). It expresses our disposition toward superiors: we must "receive with meekness the engrafted word" (James 1:21). If the wife is to be in submission to her husband, it must be in a meek and quiet spirit, which, in the sight of God, is of great value (see 1 Peter 3). As one of the fruits of the Spirit, meekness ought to characterize all our daily interaction with fellow Christians, and extend to all those we meet (see Ephesians 4:2; Galatians 5:22; Colossians 3:12; Titus 3:2). It is mentioned in Scripture along with humility because that is the inward disposition concerning oneself out of which meekness toward others springs.

There is perhaps none of the lovely virtues which adorn the image of God's Son which is more seldom seen in those who ought to be examples. There are many servants of Jesus, in whom much love to souls, much service for the salvation of others, and much zeal for God's will, are visible, and yet who continually fall short in this. This occurs most often when they are offended or hurt unexpectedly. Whether at home or abroad, they are carried away by temper and anger, and have to confess that they have lost the perfect rest of soul in God! There is no virtue, perhaps, for which some have prayed more earnestly. They would give anything if, in their fellowship with partner, children, or servants, in company or in business, they could always quiet their temper, and exhibit the meekness and gentleness of Christ. The grief and disappointment experienced by those who long for it, and yet have not discovered the secret of meekness, is unspeakable.

The self-control needed for this seems so impossible to some that they seek comfort in the belief that this blessing belongs to a certain natural temperament, and is too contrary to their character for them ever to expect it. To satisfy themselves, they find all sorts of excuses: "They do not mean to be so mean. Though the tongue or the temper is sharp, there is still love in their hearts. It would not be good to be too gentle; evil would be strengthened by it." And thus, the call to entire conformity to the holy gentleness of the Lamb of God is robbed of all its power. And the world is strengthened in its belief that Christians are, after all, not very much different from other people. Though they do indeed say, they do not show that Christ changes the heart and life after His own image. And, the soul hurts itself, and causes unspeakable harm in Christ's Church through its unfaithfulness in appropriating this blessing of salvation: the bearing of the image and likeness of God.

This grace is of great value in the sight of God. In the Old Testament, there are many glorious promises for the meek, which Jesus gathered up into this one, "Blessed are the meek, for they shall inherit the earth" (see Psalm 25:9, 76:9; Proverbs 3:34; Jeremiah 2:3). In the New Testament, its praise consists in that it is His meekness which gives supernatural, incomparable beauty to the image of our Lord. A meek spirit is of great value in God's sight; it is the choicest ornament of the Beloved Son. The Father could surely offer no higher inducement to His children to seek it above all things.

For everyone who longs to possess this spirit, Christ's word is full of comfort and encouragement: "Learn of Me, for I am meek." And what will it profit us to learn that *He is meek?* Will the experience of His meekness not make the discovery of our lack of it all the more painful? What we ask, Lord, is that You teach us how *we* may be meek. The answer is again: "Learn of Me, for I am meek."

We are in danger of seeking meekness and the other graces of our Lord Jesus as gifts which we must be conscious of, before we practice them. This is not the path of faith. "Moses knew not that the skin of his face shone" (Exodus 34:29), he had only seen the glory of God. The soul that seeks to be meek must learn that Jesus is meek. We must take time to gaze on His meekness, until the heart has received the full impression: He only is meek; with Him alone can meekness be found. When we begin to realize this, we will then fix our hearts on the truth: This meek One is *Jesus the Savior.* All He is, all He has, is for His redeemed ones. His meekness is to be communicated to us. But, He does not impart it by giving, as it were, something of it away to us. No! we must learn that He alone is meek. Only when He enters and takes possession of heart and life, does He bring His meekness with Him. It is with the meekness of Jesus that we can be meek.

We know how little He succeeded in making His disciples meek and lowly while on earth. It was because He had not yet obtained the new life, and could not yet bestow, through His resurrection, the Holy Spirit. But, now He can do it. He has since then been exalted to the power of God to reign in our hearts, to conquer every enemy, and to continue in us His own holy life. Jesus was our visible Example on earth. that we might see in Him what the hidden life that He would give us from heaven would be like, and that He Himself would be within us.

"Learn of Me, for I am meek and lowly of heart." Without ceasing, the word sounds in our ears as our Lord's answer to all the sad complaints of His redeemed ones concerning the difficulty of restraining temper. O my brethren! why is Jesus, your Jesus, your life, and your strength, the meek and lowly One, if not to impart to you, to whom He so wholly belongs, His own meekness?

Therefore, only believe! Believe that Jesus is able to fill your heart with His own spirit of meekness. Believe that Jesus Himself will, through His own Spirit, accomplish in you the work that you have in vain endeavored to do. "Behold! Thy King cometh unto thee, meek." Welcome Him to dwell in your heart. Expect Him to *reveal Himself to you.* Everything depends on this. Learn that He is meek and lowly of heart, and you *will* find rest for your soul.

Precious Savior, grant me now, under the overshadowing of the Holy Spirit, to draw near to You, and to appropriate Your heavenly meekness as my life. Lord, you have not shown me Your meekness as a Moses who demands but does not give. You are Jesus who saves from all sin, giving in its stead Your heavenly holiness. Lord, I claim Your meekness as a part of the salvation which You have given me. I cannot do without it. How can I glorify You if I do not possess it? Lord, I will learn that You are meek. Blessed Lord, teach me. And teach me that You are always with me, always in me as my life. Abiding in You, with You abiding in me, I have the meek One to help me and make me like Yourself.

O holy meekness! You have not come down to earth only for a short visit, then to disappear again in the heavens. You have come to seek a home. I offer You my heart; come and dwell in it.

Blessed Lamb of God, my Savior and Helper, I count on You. You will make Your meekness dwell in me. Through Your indwelling You conform me to Your image. O come, and as an act of your rich, free grace even now, as I wait on You, reveal Yourself as my King, meek, and coming in to take possession of me for Yourself.

"Precious, gentle, holy Jesus,
Blessed Bridegroom of my heart,
In Thy secret inner chamber,
Thou wilt show me what Thou art. Amen."

Chapter 27

LIKE CHRIST...
Abiding In The Love Of God

"As the Father hath loved me, so have I loved you: continue ye in my love. If ye keep my commandments, ye shall abide in my love; even as I have kept my Father's commandments, and abide in his love"—John 15:9-10.

Our blessed Lord not only said, "Abide in Me," but also, "Abide in My love." Of the abiding in Him, the main thing is the entering into, dwelling in, and being rooted in that wonderful love with which He loves us and gives Himself to us. "Love...seeketh not her own" (1 Corinthians 13:5). It always goes out of itself to live and be at one with the beloved. It continually opens itself and stretches its arms wide to receive and hold fast the object of its desire. Christ's love longs to possess us. The abiding in Christ is an intensely personal relationship. It is the losing of ourselves in the fellowship of an infinite love, and finding our life in the experience of being loved by Him—being nowhere at home but in His love.

To reveal this life in His love to us in all its divine beauty and blessedness, Jesus tells us that His love for us, in which we are to abide, is just the same as the Father's love for Him, in which He abides. Surely, if anything were necessary to make the abiding in His love more wonderful and attractive, this ought to do so. "As the Father loved Me, so have I loved you: continue ye in My love." Our life may be Christlike, unspeakably blessed in the consciousness of an infinite love embracing and delighting in us.

We know how this was the secret of Christ's wonderful life, and His strength in prospect of death. At His baptism, the divine message which the Spirit brought and unceasingly maintained in living power was heard, "This is My Beloved Son, in whom I am well pleased" (Matthew 3:17). More than once we read: "The Father loveth the Son" (John 3:35; 5:20). Christ speaks of it as His highest blessedness: "That the world may know that. . . Thou hast loved them, even as *Thou hast loved me. . . Thou lovedst Me* before the foundation of the world" (John 17:23,24). "That *the love wherewith Thou hast loved Me* may be in them" (John 17:26). Just as we day by day walk and live in the light of the sun shining around us, so Jesus just lived in the light of the glory of the Father's love shining on Him all the day. It was as the Beloved of God that He was able to do God's will, and finish His work. He dwelt in the love of the Father.

And just so, we are the beloved of Jesus. As the Father loved Him, He loves us. And what we need is just to take time, and, shutting our eyes to all around us, worship and wait until we see the infinite love of God in all its power and glory streaming forth on us through the heart of Jesus. It is seeking to make itself known, and to get complete possession of us—offering itself to us as our home and resting place. Oh, if the Christian would only take the time to let the wondrous thought fill him, "I am the beloved of the Lord. Jesus loves me every moment, just as the Father loved Him." Then, how our faith would grow, and we would believe that we are loved as Christ was. We must walk as He walked!

But, there is a second point in the comparison. Not only is the love we are to abide in like that in which He abode, but the way to our abiding is the same as His. As Son, Christ was in the Father's love when He came into the world. But, it was only through obedience that He could secure its continued enjoyment, and could abide in it. Nor was this an obedience that cost Him nothing. No, it was in giving up His own will, learning obedience by what He suffered, becoming obedient unto death—even the death of the cross—that He kept the Father's commandments and *abode in His love*. "Therefore doth My Father love Me, *because* I lay down My life.... This *commandment* have I received of My Father" (John 10:17,18). "The Father hath not left Me alone; *for I do* always those things that please Him" (John 8:29). And having thus given us His example, and proved how surely the path of obedience takes us up into the presence and love and glory of God, He invites us to follow Him. "If ye keep My commandments, ye shall abide in My love, *even as* I kept My Father's commandments, and abide in His love."

Christlike obedience is the way to a Christlike enjoyment of divine love. How it secures our boldness of access into God's presence! "Let us love *in deed and in truth, and hereby* we know that we are of the truth, and shall assure our hearts before Him" "Beloved! if our heart condemn us not, then have we *confidence toward God.* And whatsoever we ask, we receive of Him, *because we keep His commandments,* and do those things that are pleasing in His sight" (1 John 3:21-22). How it gives us boldness before men, and lifts us above their approval or contempt because we move at God's bidding, and feel that we have but to obey orders! And what boldness, too, in the face of difficulty or danger! We are doing God's will, and dare leave to Him all responsibility as to failure or success. The heart filled with the thought of direct and entire obedience to God alone rises above the world into the will of God—into the place where God's love rests on him. Like Christ, he has his abode in the love of God.

Let us seek to learn from Christ what it means to have this spirit of obedience ruling our life. It implies the spirit of dependence—the confession that we have neither the right nor the desire in anything to do our own will. It involves teachableness of spirit. Conscious of the blinding influence of tradition, prejudice, and habit, it does not take its law from men, but from God Himself. Conscious of how little the most careful study of the Word can reveal God's will in its spiritual power, it seeks to be led, and, for this reason, to be entirely under the rule of the Holy Spirit. It knows that its views of truth and duty are very partial and deficient, and counts on being led by God Himself to deeper insight and higher attainment.

The spirit of obedience has marked God's word, "If thou wilt diligently hearken to the voice of the Lord thy God, and wilt do that which is right in His sight" (Exodus 15:26). It has understood that it is only when the commands do not come from conscience, memory, or the book, but from the *living voice* of the Lord heard speaking through the Spirit, that the obedience will be possible and acceptable. It sees that it is only by following the Father's personal directions, and by service rendered to Him, that obedience has its full value and brings its full blessing. The spirit of obedience takes great care to live on the altar, given up to God—to keep eye and ear open to God for every indication of His blessed will. It is not content with doing right for its own sake. It brings everything in personal relationship to God Himself, doing it as unto the Lord. This obedience wants every hour and every step in life to be a fellowship with God. It longs, in little things and daily life, to be consciously obeying the Father, because this is the only way to be prepared for higher work. Its one desire is the glory of God in the triumph of His will. The spirit of obedience has one means for obtaining that desire—with all its heart and strength, it must work out that will each moment of the day. And its one but sufficient reward is this—it knows that through the will of God lies the road, opened up by Christ Himself, deeper into the love of God: "If ye keep My commandments, ye shall abide in My love."

Oh, this blessed, Christlike obedience, leading to a Christlike abiding in the divine love! To attain it, we must study Christ more. He emptied Himself, humbled Himself, and *became obedient.* May He empty us and humble us, too! He *learned obedience* in the school of God, and being made perfect, became the author of eternal salvation to all *who obey Him.* We must yield ourselves to be taught obedience by Him! We need to listen to what He has told us about how He did nothing of Himself, but only what He saw and heard from the Father. Entire dependence and continual waiting on the Father was the root of His implicit obedience, and this again the secret of ever growing knowledge of the Father's deeper secrets (see John 5:19-20). God's love and man's obedience are like the lock and key fitting into each other. It is God's grace that has fitted the key to the lock; it is man who uses the key to unlock the treasures of love.

In the light of Christ's example and words, what new meaning comes to God's words spoken to His people from of old! "In blessing I will bless thee, and in multiplying I will multiply thy seed... *because thou hast obeyed My voice"* (Genesis 23:17,18). "If ye will *obey My voice* indeed. . . ye shall be a peculiar treasure unto Me" (Exodus 19:5). "The Lord shall *greatly bless thee*. . . if thou *carefully hearken* unto the voice of the Lord thy God, to observe to do all these commandments" (Deuteronomy 15:4,5). Love and obedience indeed become the two great factors in the wonderful communion between God and man. The love of God is the giving of Himself and all He has to man. The obedience of the believer in that love is the giving of himself and all he has to God.

We have heard a good deal in these later years of full surrender and entire consecration, and thousands praise God for all the blessing He has given them through these words. Only let us beware that we are not led too much, in connection with them, to seek for a blessed experience to be enjoyed, or a state to be maintained, while the simple, downright doing of God's will to which they point is overlooked. Let us take hold and use this word which God loves to use: obedience. "To obey is better than sacrifice" (1 Samuel 15:22). Self-sacrifice is nothing without—is nothing but—obedience. It was the meek and lowly obedience of Christ, as of a servant and a son, that made His sacrifice such a sweet-smelling savor. It is humble, childlike obedience, first gently listening to the *Father's voice,* and then doing that which is right *in His sight*, that will bring us the witness that we please Him.

Dear reader! will this not be our life? So simple and sublime is obeying Jesus, and abiding in His love.

O my God! what will I say to the wonderful interchange between the life of heaven and the life of earth You have set before me? Your Son, our blessed Lord, has shown and proved to us how it is possible on this earth of ours, and how unspeakably blessed, for a man to live with the love of God always surrounding him, by just yielding himself to obey Your voice and will. And, because He is ours, our Head and our Life, we know that we can indeed live and walk as we see Him do. Our souls may always be abiding and rejoicing in Your divine love, because You accept our feeble keeping of Your commandments for His sake. O my God, it is indeed too wonderful that we are called to this Christlike dwelling in love through the Christlike obedience Your Spirit works!

Blessed Jesus! how can I praise You for coming and bringing such a life on earth and making me a sharer in it? O my Lord! I can only yield myself afresh to You to keep Your commandments, as You kept the Father's. Lord! only impart to me the secret of Your own blessed obedience: the open ear, the watchful eye, the meek and lowly heart, the childlike giving up of all as the beloved Son to the beloved Father. Savior! fill my heart with Your love. In the faith and experience of that love, I will do it, too. Yes, Lord, this only be my life—keeping Your commandments, and abiding in Your love. Amen.

Chapter 28

LIKE CHRIST...
Led By The Spirit

"And Jesus being full of the Holy Ghost returned from Jordan, and was led by the Spirit into the wilderness"—Luke 4:1.

"Be filled with the Spirit"—Ephesians 5:18.

"For as many as are led by the Spirit of God, they are the sons of God"—Romans 8:14.

From His very birth, the Lord Jesus had the Spirit dwelling in Him. But, there were times when He needed special communications of the Spirit from the Father. Thus it was with His baptism. The descent of the Holy Spirit on Him—the baptism of the Spirit, given in the baptism with water—was a real transaction: He was filled with the Spirit. He returned from the Jordan full of the Holy Spirit, and experienced more manifestly than ever the leading of the Spirit. In the wilderness, He wrestled and conquered, not in His own divine power, but as a man who was strengthened and led by the Holy Spirit. In this also "In all things it behoved Him to be made like unto His brethren" (Hebrews 2:17).

The opposite of this truth also holds good: the brethren are in all things made like unto Him. They are called to live like Him. This is not demanded from them without their having the same power. This power is the Holy Spirit dwelling in us, whom we have of God. Even as Jesus was filled with the Spirit, and then led by the Spirit, so must we also be filled with the Spirit and be led by the Spirit.

More than once, in our meditations on the different traits of Christ's character, it has seemed almost impossible to be like Him. We have lived so little for it. We feel so little able to live thus. Let us take courage in the thought: Jesus Himself could only live thus through the Spirit. It was after He was filled with the Spirit that He was led forth by that Spirit to the place of conflict and of victory. And this blessing is ours as surely as it was His. We may be filled with the Spirit; we may be led by the Spirit. Jesus, who was Himself baptized with the Spirit to set an example of how we are to live, has ascended into heaven to baptize us into likeness with Himself, He who would live like Jesus must begin here: He must be baptized with the Spirit. What God demands from His children He first gives. He demands entire likeness to Christ because He will give us, as He did Jesus, the fullness of the Spirit. We must be filled with the Spirit.

Here we have the reason why the teaching of the imitation and likeness to Christ has so little prominence in His Church. Men sought it in their own strength, with the help of some workings of the Holy

Spirit. They did not understand that nothing less than being filled with the Spirit was needed. No wonder they thought that real conformity to Christ could not be expected of us, because they had mistaken thoughts about being *filled with the Spirit.* It was thought to be the privilege of a few, and not the calling and duty of *every child of God.* It was not sufficiently realized that "Be ye filled with the Spirit" is a command to every Christian. Only when the Church first gives the baptism of the Spirit, and Jesus, as the Savior, *baptizes with the Spirit* each one who believes in Him, only then will likeness to Christ be sought after and attained. People will then understand and acknowledge: to be like Christ we must be led by the same Spirit; and, to be led by the Spirit as He was, we must be filled with the Spirit. Nothing less than the fullness of the Spirit is absolutely necessary to live a truly Christian, Christlike life.

The way to arrive at it is simple. It is Jesus who baptizes with the Spirit. He who comes to Him desiring it will get it. All that He requires of us is the surrender of faith to receive what He gives.

The surrender of faith. What He asks is whether or not we are indeed in earnest to follow in His footsteps, and for this to be baptized of the Spirit. Do not let there be any hesitation as to our answer. First, look back on all the glorious promises of His love and of His Spirit, in which the blessed privilege is set forth: Even as I, ye also. Remember that it was of this likeness to Himself in everything that He said to the Father: "The glory which Thou gavest Me I have given them" (John 17:22). Think how the love of Christ and the true desire to please Him—how the glory of God and the needs of the world—plead with us not, through our laziness, to despise the heavenly birthright of being Christlike. Acknowledge the sacred right of ownership Christ has in you, His blood-bought ones. And, let nothing prevent you from answering: "Yes, dear Lord, as far as is allowed to a child of dust, I will be like You. I am entirely Yours. I must, I will, in all things bear Your image. It is for this that I ask to be filled with the Spirit."

The surrender of faith—only this, and nothing less that this, does He demand. Let us give what He asks. If we yield ourselves to be like Him in all things, let it be in the quiet trust that He accepts, and at once begins in secret to make the Spirit work more mightily in us. Let us believe it although we do not immediately experience it. To be filled with the Holy Spirit, we must wait on our Lord in faith. We can depend on the fact that His love desires to give us more than we know. Let our surrender be made in this assurance.

And, let this surrender of faith be entire. The fundamental law of following Christ is this: "He who loses his life shall find it." The Holy Spirit comes to take away the old life, and to give, in its place, the life of Christ in you. Renounce the old life of self-working and self-watching, and believe that, as the air you breathe renews your life every moment, so naturally and continually the Holy Spirit will renew your life. In the work of the Holy Spirit in you, there are no breaks or interruptions. You are in the Spirit as your vital air, and the Spirit is in you as your life breath. Through the Spirit, God works in you both to will and to do according to His good pleasure.

Oh, Christian, have a deep reverence for the work of the Spirit who dwells within you. Believe in God's power, which works in you through the Spirit, to conform you to Christ's life and image moment by moment. Be occupied with Jesus and His life, in the full assurance that the Holy Spirit knows, in deep quiet, to fulfill His office of communicating Jesus to you. That life is, simultaneously, your example and your strength. Remember that the fullness of the Spirit is yours in Jesus. It is a real gift which you accept and hold in faith, even when you do not feel its presence, and on which you count to work in you all that you need. The feeling may be weakness, fear, and much trembling, and yet the speaking, working, and living may be in demonstration of the Spirit and of power (see 1 Corinthians 2:3-4).

Live in the faith that the fullness of the Spirit is yours, and that you will not be disappointed if, looking to Jesus, you rejoice every day in the blessed trust that the care of your spiritual life is in the hands of the Holy Spirit the Comforter. Thus, with the loving presence of Jesus in you, the living likeness to Jesus will be seen on you. With the Spirit of life in Christ Jesus dwelling within, the likeness of the life of Christ Jesus will shine around.

And, if it does not appear that in thus believing

and obeying your desires are fulfilled, remember that it is in the fellowship with the members of Christ's body, and in the full surrender to Christ's service in the world, that the full power of the Spirit is made manifest. It was when Jesus gave Himself to enter into full fellowship with men around Him, and like them to be baptized with water, that He was baptized with the Holy Spirit. And, it was when He had given Himself in His second baptism of suffering, a sacrifice for us, that He received the Holy Spirit to give to us. Seek fellowship with God's children, who will pray with you and believe for the baptism of the Spirit. The disciples received the Spirit not singly, but when they were with one accord in one place. Band yourself with God's children around you to work for souls. The Spirit is the power from on high to prepare you for that work. The promise will be fulfilled to the believing, willing servants who want Him not for their enjoyment, but for that work.

Christ was filled with the Spirit so that He would be able to work and live and die for us. Give yourself to such a Christlike living and dying for men, and you may depend on a Christlike baptism of the Spirit, a Christlike fullness of the Spirit, to be your portion.

Blessed Lord! how wondrously You have provided for our growing likeness to Yourself, in giving us Your own Holy Spirit. You have told us that it is His work to reveal You, to give us Your real presence within us. It is by Him that all You have won for us, all the life and holiness and strength we see in You, is brought over and imparted and made our very own. He takes of Yours, shows it to us, and makes it ours. Blessed Jesus! we do thank You for the gift of the Holy Spirit.

And now, we beseech You, fill us, fill us full, with the Holy Spirit! Lord! nothing less is sufficient. We cannot be led like You, we cannot fight and conquer like You, we cannot love and serve like You, we cannot live and die like You, unless like You we are full of the Holy Spirit. Blessed, blessed be Your name! You have commanded, You have promised it—it may, it can, it will be.

Holy Savior! draw your disciples together to wait and plead for this. Let their eyes be opened to see the wondrous unfulfilled promises of floods of the Holy Spirit. Let their hearts be drawn to give themselves, like You, to live and die for men. And we know it will be Your delight to fulfill Your office, as He that baptizes with the Holy Spirit and with fire. Glory be to Your name. Amen.

Chapter 29

LIKE CHRIST...
In His Life Through The Father

"I live by the Father: so he that eateth me, even he shall live by me"—John 6:57.

Every contemplation of a walk in the footsteps of Christ, and in His likeness, reveals anew the need of concentrating on the deep, living union between the Forerunner and His followers. *Like Christ:* the longer we meditate on the word, the more we realize how impossible it is without that other: *In Christ.* The outward likeness can only be the manifestation of a living, inward union. To do the same works as Christ, I must have the same life. The more earnestly I take Him for my Example, the more I am driven to Him as my Head. Only an inner life essentially like His can lead us to a visible walk like His.

What a blessed word we have here, to assure us that His life on earth and ours are really like each other: "I live by the Father: *so* he that eateth Me, even he shall live by Me." If you desire to understand your life in Christ—what He will be for you and how He will work in you—you only have to contemplate what the Father was for Him, and how He worked in Him. Christ's life in and through the Father is the image and the measure of what your life in and through the Son may be. Let us meditate on this.

As Christ's life was a life *hidden in God in heaven,* so must ours be. When He emptied Himself of His divine glory, He laid aside the free use of His divine attributes. He thus needed, as a man, to live by faith. He needed to wait on the Father for such communications of wisdom and power as it pleased the Father to impart to Him. He was entirely dependent on the Father; His life was hid in God. Not in virtue of His own independent Godhead, but through the operations of the Holy Spirit, did He speak and act as the Father from time to time taught Him.

Exactly so, believer, must your life be hid with Christ in God. Let this encourage you. Christ calls you to a life of faith and dependence, because it is the life He Himself led. He has tried it and proved its blessedness. He is willing now to live over again His life in you, to teach you also to live in no other way. He knew that the Father was His life, that He lived through the Father, and that the Father supplied His need moment by moment. And now, He assures you that as He lived through the Father, even so you will live through Him. Take this assurance in faith. Let your heart be filled with the thought of the blessedness of this fullness of life, which is prepared for you in Christ, and will be abundantly supplied as you need it. Do not think of your spiritual life as something that you must watch over and nourish with care and anxiety. Rejoice every day that you need not live on your own strength, but in your Lord Jesus, even as He lived through His Father.

Even as Christ's life was *a life of divine power,* although a life of dependence, so ours *will also be.* He never repented having laid aside His glory to live before God as a man upon earth. The Father never disappointed His confidence; He gave Him all He needed to accomplish His work. Christ experienced that, blessed as it was to be like God in heaven and to dwell in the enjoyment of divine perfection, it was no less blessed to live in entire dependence on earth, and to receive everything day by day from His hands.

Believer, if you will let it be so, your life can be the same. The divine power of the Lord Jesus will work in and through us. Do not think that your earthly circumstances make a holy life to God's glory impossible. Christ came and lived on earth just to manifest, in the midst of earthly surroundings which were even more difficult, the divine life. As He lived so blessed an earthly life through the Father, so you may also live your earthly life through Him. Only cultivate large expectations of what the Lord will do for you. Let it be your sole desire to attain to an entire union with Him. *It is impossible to say what the Lord Jesus would do for a soul who is truly willing to live as entirely through Him as He through the Father.* Because, just as He lived through the Father, and the Father made that life with all its work so glorious, so you will experience, in all your work, how entirely He has undertaken to work all in you.

As the life of Christ was *the manifestation of His real union with the Father, so ours also.* Christ says, "As the living Father hath sent Me, and I live by the Father" (John 6:57). When the Father desired to manifest Himself on earth in His love, He could intrust that work to no one less than His beloved Son, who was one with Him. It was because He was *Son* that the Father sent Him. It was because the Father had sent Him that it could not be otherwise—He must care for His life. The blessed certainty that Jesus would live on earth through the Father rested in the union upon which the mission depended.

"Even so," Christ said, "He that eateth Me, he shall live by Me." He had said before, "He that eateth My flesh, and drinketh My blood, dwelleth in Me, and I in him" (John 6:56). In death, He had given His flesh and blood for the life of the world. Through faith, the soul partakes of the power of His death and resurrection, and receives its right to His life, as He had a right to His Father's life. In the words, "Whosoever eateth Me," is expressed the intimate union and unbroken communion with the Lord Jesus, which is the power of a life in Him. The one great work for the soul, who truly longs to live entirely and only by Christ, is to eat Him, to daily feed on Him, and to make Him his own.

To attain this, continually seek to have your heart filled with a believing and lively assurance that all Christ's fullness of life is truly yours. Rejoice in the contemplation of His humanity in heaven, and the wonderful provision God has made through the Holy Spirit for the communication of this life of your Head in heaven to flow unbroken and unhindered down upon you. Thank God unceasingly for the redemption in which He opened the way to the life of God, and for the wonderful life now provided for you in the Son. Offer yourself unreservedly to Him with an open heart and consecrated life that seeks His service alone. In such trust and consecration of faith, in the outpouring of love and cultivation of communion, with His words abiding in you, let Jesus be your daily food. He who eats Me shall live by Me: even as the Father has sent Me, and I live by the Father.

Beloved Christian! what do you think? The imitation of Christ begins to seem possible in the light of this promise. He who lives through Christ can also live like Him. Therefore, let this wonderful life of Christ on earth through the Father be the object of our adoring contemplation, until our whole heart understands and accepts the word, "So, he that eateth Me, even he shall live by Me" (John 6:57). Then, we will dismiss all care and anxiety, because the same Christ who set us the example also works in us from heaven that life which can live out the example. And, our life will become a continual song: To Him who lives in us, in order that we may live like Him, be the love and praise of our hearts. Amen.

O my God! how can I thank You for this wonderful grace! Your Son became man to teach us the blessedness of a life of human dependence on the Father; He lived through the Father. It has been given us to see in Him how the divine life can live, work, and conquer on earth. And now, He is ascended into heaven, and has all power to let that life work in us. We are called to live even as He did on earth: we live through Him. O God, praised be Your name for this unspeakable grace.

Lord, my God, hear the prayer that I now offer to You. If it may be, show me more, much more, of Christ's life through the Father. I need to know it, O my God, if I am to live as He did! Oh, give me the spirit of wisdom in the knowledge of Him. Then, I will know what I may expect from Him, what I can do through Him. It will then no longer be a struggle and an effort to live according to Your will and His example. Because I will then know that His blessed life on earth is now mine, according to the word, "Even as I through the Father, so ye through Me." Then, I will daily feed upon Christ in the joyful experience: I live through Him. O my Father! grant this in full measure for His name's sake. Amen.

Chapter 30

LIKE CHRIST...
In Glorifying The Father

"Father, the hour is come; glorify thy Son, that thy Son also may glorify thee.... I have glorified thee on the earth"—John 17:1,4.

"Herein is my Father glorified, that ye bear much fruit; so shall ye be my disciples"—John 15:8.

The glory of an object is that its intrinsic worth and excellence answers perfectly to all that is expected of it. That excellence or perfection may be so hidden or unknown that the object has no glory to those who behold it. To *glorify* is to remove every hindrance, and so to reveal the full worth and perfection of the object, that its glory is seen and acknowledged by all.

The highest perfection of God, and the deepest mystery of the Godhead, is His holiness. In it, righteousness and love are united. As the Holy One, He hates and condemns sin. As the Holy One, He also frees the sinner from its power, and raises him to communion with Himself. His name is, "The Holy One of Israel, thy Redeemer" (Isaiah 47:4). The song of redemption is: "Great is the Holy One of Israel in the midst of thee" (Isaiah 12:6). The title of Holy in the New Testament belongs more to the blessed Spirit, whose special work is to maintain the fellowship of God with man, than to the Father or the Son. It is this holiness, judging sin and saving sinners, which is the glory of God. For this reason the two words are often found together. So in the song of Moses: "Who is like Thee, *glorious in holiness?"* (Exodus 15:11). So in the song of the Seraphim: *"Holy, Holy, Holy,* is the Lord of hosts: the whole earth is full of His *glory*" (Isaiah 6:3). And so in the song of the Lamb: "Who shall not . . . *glorify* Thy Name? for Thou only art *holy*" (Revelation 15:4). As has been well said: "God's *glory* is His manifested holiness; God's holiness is His hidden *glory."*

When Jesus came to earth, it was that He might glorify the Father, and that He might again show forth, in its true light and beauty, that glory which sin had so entirely hid from man. Man himself had been created in the image of God, that God might lay His glory upon him, to be shown forth in him—that God might be glorified in him. The Holy Spirit says, "Man is the image and glory of God" (1 Corinthians 11:7). Jesus came to restore man to his high destiny. He laid aside the glory which He had with the Father, and came in our weakness and humiliation, that He might teach us how to glorify the Father on earth. God's glory is perfect and infinite. Man cannot contribute any new glory to God, above what He has: he can only serve as a glass in which the glory of

God is reflected. God's holiness is His glory. As this holiness of God is seen in mankind, God is glorified; His glory as God is shown forth.

Jesus glorified God *by obeying Him.* In giving His commandments to Israel, God continually said, "Be ye holy, for I am holy" (Leviticus 11:44). In keeping them, they would be transformed into a life of harmony with Him, they would enter into fellowship with Him as the Holy One. In His conflict with sin and Satan, in His sacrifice of His own will, in His waiting for the Father's teaching, in His unquestioning obedience to the Word, Christ showed that He counted nothing worth living for, except that men might understand what a blessed thing it is to let this holy God really be God. His will alone acknowledged and obeyed. Because He alone is holy, His will alone should be done, and so His glory be shown in us.

Jesus glorified God *by confessing Him.* In His teaching, He did more than make known the message God had given Him, and show us who the Father is. There is something far more striking. He continually spoke of His own personal relationship to the Father. He did not trust to the silent influence of His holy life. He wanted men to distinctly understand what the root and aim of that life was. Time after time, He told them that He came as a servant sent from the Father, that He depended on Him and owed everything to Him, that He only sought the Father's honor, and that all His happiness was to please the Father, to secure His love and favor.

Jesus glorified God *by giving Himself for the work of His redeeming love.* God's glory is His holiness, and God's holiness is His redeeming love—love that triumphs over sin by conquering the sin and rescuing the sinner. Jesus not only told of the Father being the Righteous One, whose condemnation must rest on sin, and the Loving One, who saves everyone who turns from his sin, but He gave Himself to be a sacrifice to that righteousness, a servant to that love, even unto death. It was not only in acts of obedience or words of confession that He glorified God, but in giving Himself to magnify the holiness of God, to vindicate His law and His love by His atonement. He gave Himself—His whole life and being, Himself wholly—to show how the Father loved and longed to bless, how the Father must condemn the sin, and yet would save the sinner. He counted nothing too great a sacrifice. He lived and died only for this—that the glory of the Father, the glory of His holiness, of His redeeming love, might break through the dark veil of sin and flesh, and shine into the hearts of the children of men. As He Himself expressed it in the last week of His life, when the approaching anguish began to press in upon Him: "Now is My soul troubled; and what shall I say? Father, save Me from this hour? but for this cause came I unto this hour. Father! glorify Thy name" (John 12:27-28). And the assurance came that the sacrifice was well-pleasing and accepted, in the answer: "I have both glorified it, and will glorify it again" (John 12:28).

It was thus that Jesus, as a man, was prepared to take part in the glory of God: He sought it in the humiliation on earth; He found it on the throne of heaven. And so, He is our forerunner, leading many children to glory. He shows us that the sure way to the glory of God in heaven is to live only for the glory of God on earth. Yes, this is the glory of a life on earth. Glorifying God here, we are prepared to be glorified with Him forever.

Beloved Christian! is it not a wonderful calling, blessed beyond all conception, like Christ to live only to glorify God, to let God's glory shine out in every part of our life? Let us take time to take in the wondrous thought: our daily life, down to its most ordinary acts, may be transparent with the glory of God. Oh! let us study this trait as one that makes the wondrous image of our Jesus especially attractive to us: He glorified the Father. Let us listen to Him as He points us to the high aim, *that your Father in heaven may be glorified,* and as He shows us the way, *Herein is my Father glorified.* Let us remember how He told us that, when in heaven He answers our prayer, this would still be His object. And, let it, in every breathing of prayer and faith, be our object, too: *"That the Father may be glorified in the Son."* Let our whole life, like Christ's, be animated by this as its ruling principle, growing stronger until in a holy enthusiasm our watchword has become: *All, all to the glory of God.* And, let our faith firmly hold onto the confidence that, in the fullness of the Spirit, there is the sure provision for our desire being fulfilled: "Know ye not that your body is the temple of the Holy Ghost which is in you. . . therefore glorify God in your holy body, and in your spirit" (1 Corinthians 6:19,20).

If we want to know the way, let us again study Jesus. He obeyed the Father. Let simple, downright obedience mark our whole life. Let a humble, childlike waiting for direction, a soldier-like looking for orders, a Christlike dependence on the Father's showing us His way, be our daily attitude. Let everything be done to the Lord, according to His will, for His glory, in direct relationship to Himself. Let God's glory shine out in the holiness of our life.

He confessed the Father. He did not hesitate to speak often of His personal relationship and communion, just as a little child would do of an earthly parent. It is not enough that we live right before men: how can they understand, if there is no interpreter? They need, not as a matter of preaching, but as a personal testimony, to hear that what we are and do is *because we love the Father, and are living for Him*. The witness of the life and the words must go together.

And He gave Himself to the Father's work. So He glorified Him. He showed sinners that God has a right to have us wholly and only for Himself, that God's glory alone is worth living and dying for, and that as we give ourselves to this, God will most wonderfully use and bless us in leading others to see and confess His glory, too. It was that men might glorify the Father in heaven, might find their blessedness also in knowing and serving this glorious God, that Jesus lived, and that we must live, too. Oh! let us give ourselves to God for men. Let us plead and work and live and die, that men, our fellow-men, may see that God is glorious in holiness, that the whole earth may be filled with His glory.

Believer! "the Spirit of glory and of God resteth upon you" (1 Peter 4:14). Jesus delights to do in you His beloved work of glorifying the Father. Fear not to say: O my Father, in Your Son, *like Your Son,* I will only live to glorify You.

O my God! I do pray You, show me Your glory! I feel deeply how utterly impossible it is, by any resolution or effort of mine, to lift myself up or bind myself to live for Your glory alone. But if You will reveal unto me Your glory, if You will make all Your goodness pass before me, and show me how glorious You are, how there is no glory but Yours; if, O my Father! You will let Your glory shine into my heart, and take possession of my innermost being, I never will be able to do anything but glorify You—but live to make known what a glorious, holy God You are.

Lord Jesus! who came to earth to glorify the Father in our sight, and ascend to heaven leaving us to do it now in Your name and stead, oh! give us, by the Holy Spirit, a sight of how You did it. Teach us the meaning of Your obedience to the Father, Your acknowledgement that, at any cost, His will must be done. Teach us to mark Your confession of the Father, and how You did, in personal testimony, tell men of what He was to You, and what you feel for Him, and let our lips, too, tell what we taste of the love of the Father, that men may glorify Him. And above all, oh! teach us that it is in saving sinners that redeeming love has its triumph and its joy, that it is in holiness casting out sin that God has His highest glory. And do so take possession of our whole hearts that we may love and labor, live and die, for this one thing, "That every tongue should confess that Jesus Christ is Lord, *to the glory of God the Father"* (Philippians 2:11).

O my Father! let the whole earth, let my heart, be filled with Your glory. Amen.

Chapter 31

LIKE CHRIST...
In His Glory

"We know that, when he shall appear, we shall be like him; for we shall see him as he is. And every man that hath this hope in him purifieth himself, even as he is pure"—1 John 3:2-3.

"And I appoint unto you a kingdom, as my Father hath appointed unto me"—Luke 22:29.

God's glory is His holiness. To glorify God is to yield ourselves so that God may show forth His glory in us. It is only by yielding ourselves to be holy, to let His holiness fill our life, that His glory can shine forth from us. The one work of Christ was to glorify the Father, to reveal what a glorious, holy God He is. Our one work is, like Christ's, so by our obedience, testimony, and life, to make known our God as "glorious in holiness" (Exodus 15:11), that He may be glorified in heaven and earth.

When the Lord Jesus had glorified the Father on earth, the Father glorified Him with Himself in heaven. This was not only His just reward, it was a necessity in the very nature of things. There is no other place for a life given up to the glory of God, as Christ's was, than in that glory. The law holds good for us, too. A heart that yearns and thirsts for the glory of God, that is ready to live and die for it, becomes prepared and fitted to live in it. *Living to God's glory* on earth is the gate to *living in God's glory* in heaven. If with Christ we glorify the Father, the Father will with Christ glorify us, too. Yes, we will be like Him in His glory.

We will be like Him in *His spiritual glory*, the glory of His holiness. In the union of the two words in the name of the Holy Spirit, we see that what is *holy* and what is *spiritual* stand in close connection with each other. When Jesus, as man, had glorified God by revealing, honoring, and giving Himself up to His holiness, He was, as man, taken up into and made partaker of the divine glory.

And so it will be with us. If here on earth we have given ourselves to have God's glory take possession of us, and if God's holiness and His Holy Spirit dwell and shine in us, then our human nature, with all our faculties, created in the likeness of God, will have poured into and transfused through it—in a way that passes all conception—the purity, the holiness, the life, and the very brightness of the glory of God.

We will be like Him *in His glorified body.* It has been well said: Embodiment is the end of the ways of God. The creation of man was to be God's masterpiece. There had previously been spirits without bodies, and animated bodies without spirits. But, in man there was to be a spirit in a body lifting up and spiritualizing the body into its own heavenly purity and perfection. Man as a whole is God's image, his body as much as his spirit. In Jesus, a human body—O mystery of mysteries!—is set upon the throne of God, is found a worthy partner and container of the divine glory. Our bodies are going to be the objects of the most astonishing miracle of divine transforming power. "He shall change our vile body, that it may be fashioned like unto His glorious body, according to the working whereby He is able even to subdue all things unto Himself" (Philippians 3:21). The glory of God as seen in our bodies, made like Christ's glorious body, will be something almost more wonderful than in our spirits. We are "waiting for the adoption, to wit, the redemption of our body" (Romans 8:23).

We will be like Him *in His place of honor*. Every object must have a proper place for its glory to be seen. Christ's place is the central one in the universe: the throne of God. He said to His disciples, "Where I am, there shall also My servant be: if any man serve Me, him will My Father honor" (John 12:26). "I appoint unto you a kingdom, as My Father hath appointed unto Me; that ye may eat and drink at My table in My kingdom, and sit on thrones judging the twelve tribes of Israel" (Luke 22:29-30). To the Church at Thyatira He says: "He that overcometh and keepeth My works unto the end, to him will I give power over the nations. . . even as I received of My Father" (Revelation 2:26,27). And to the Church at Laodicea: "To him that overcometh will I grant to sit with Me in My throne, even as I also overcame, and am set down with My Father in His throne" (Revelation 3:21). Higher and closer it cannot be: "As we have borne the image of the earthly, we shall also bear the image of the heavenly" (1 Corinthians 15:49). The likeness will be complete and perfect.

Such divine God-given glimpses into the future reveal to us, more than all our thinking, what intense truth, what divine meaning, there is in God's creative word: "Let us make man in Our image, after Our likeness" (Genesis 1:26). To show forth the likeness of the invisible, to be partaker of the divine nature, to share with God His rule of the universe, is man's destiny. His place is indeed one of unspeakable glory. Standing between two eternities—the eternal purpose in which we were predestinated to be conformed to the image of the first-born Son, and the eternal realization of that purpose when we will be like Him in His glory—we hear the voice from every side: O image-bearers of God! on the way to share the glory of God and of Christ! live a Godlike, live a Christlike, life!

"I shall be satisfied, when I awake, with Thy likeness" (Psalm 17:15), so the Psalmist sung of old. Nothing can satisfy the soul but God's image, because it was created for that. And this is not as something external to it, only seen but not possessed. It is as partaker of that likeness that we will be satisfied. Blessed are they who long for it with insatiable hunger; they shall be filled. This, the very likeness of God, will be the glory streaming down on them from God Himself, streaming through their whole being, streaming out from them through the universe. "When Christ, who is our life, shall appear, then shall ye also appear with Him in glory" (Colossians 3:4).

Beloved fellow Christians! nothing can be made manifest in that day that does not have a real existence here in this life. If the glory of God is not our life here, it cannot be hereafter. It is impossible. Only he who glorifies God here can God glorify hereafter. "Man is the image and glory of God." It is as you bear the image of God here, as you live in the likeness of Jesus—who is the brightness of His glory and the express image of His person—that you will be fitted for the glory to come. If we are to be as the image of the heavenly, Christ in glory, we must first bear the image of the earthly, Christ in humiliation.

Child of God! Christ is the uncreated image of God. Man is His created image. On the throne in glory, the two will be eternally one. You know what Christ did, how He drew near, how He sacrificed all, to restore us to the possession of that image. Oh, will we not yield ourselves at length to this wonderful love, to this glory inconceivable, and give our life wholly to manifest the likeness and the glory of Christ? Will we not, like Him, make the Father's glory our aim and hope, living to His glory here, as the way to live in His glory there?

The Father's glory: it is in this that Christ's glory and ours have their common origin. Let *the Father* be to us what He was to Him, and the Father's glory will be ours as it is His. All the traits of the life of Christ converge to this as their center. He was Son. He lived as Son; God was to Him Father. As Son, He sought the Father's glory; as Son, He found it. Oh! let this be our conformity to the image of the Son, that *the Father* is the all in all of our life. The Father's glory must be our everlasting home.

Beloved brethren! who have accompanied me thus far in these meditations on the image of our Lord, and the Christlike life in which it is to be reflected, the time is now come for us to part. Let us do so with the word, "We shall be like Him; for we shall see Him as He is. Every man that hath this hope in Him purifieth himself, even as He is pure" (1 John 3:2-3). *Like Christ!* let us pray that this may be the one aim of our faith, the one desire of our heart, the one joy of our life. Oh, what it will be when we meet in glory, when we see Him as He is, and see each other all like Him!

Ever blessed and most glorious God! what thanks we will render You for the glorious gospel of Christ, who is the image of God, and for the light of Your glory which shines upon us in Him! And, what thanks we will render You, that in Jesus we have seen the image not only of You, but of our glory, the pledge of what we are to be with You through eternity!

O God! forgive us, forgive us for Jesus' blood's sake, that we have so little believed this, that we have so little lived this. And, we beseech You that You would reveal, to all who have had fellowship with each other in these meditations, the glory in which they are to live eternally, in which they can be living even now, as they glorify You. O Father! awaken us and all Your children to see and feel what Your purpose with us is. We are indeed to spend eternity in Your glory. Your glory is to be around us and on us and in us. We are to be like Your Son in His glory. Father! we beseech You, oh visit Your Church! Let your Holy Spirit, the Spirit of glory, work mightily in her. And, let this be her one desire, the one mark by which she is known: the glory of God resting upon her.

Our Father! grant it for Jesus' sake. Amen.

On Preaching Christ Our Example

"Let us make man in Our image, after Our likeness" (Genesis 1:26). In these words of the Council of Creation, with which the Bible history of man opens, we have the revelation of the eternal purpose to which man owes his existence—the glorious, eternal future to which he is destined. God proposes to make a Godlike creature, a being who will be His very image and likeness, the visible manifestation of the glory of the Invisible One.

To have a being, at once created and yet Godlike, was indeed a task worthy of infinite wisdom. It is the nature and glory of God that He is absolutely independent of all else, having life in Himself, owing His existence to none but Himself alone. If man is to be Godlike, he must bear His image and likeness in this, too—he must become what he is to be of his own free choice. He must make himself. It is the nature and glory of man to be dependent, to owe everything to the blessed Creator. How can the contradiction be reconciled—a being at once dependent and yet self-determined, created and yet Godlike. In man, the mystery is solved. As man, God gives him life, but endows him with the wonderful power of a free will. It is only in the process of a personal and voluntary appropriation that anything so high and holy as likeness to God can really become his very own.

When sin entered and man fell from his high destiny, God did not give up His purpose. Of His revelation in Israel, the central thought was: "Be ye holy; for I am holy" (Leviticus 11:44). Likeness to God in that which constitutes His highest perfection is to be Israel's hope. Redemption had no higher ideal than Creation had revealed. It could only take up and work out the eternal purpose.

It was with this in mind that the Father sent to the earth the Son who was the express image of His person. In Him, the Godlikeness to which we had been created, and which we had personally to appropriate and make our own, was revealed in human form. He came to show us the image of God and our own image. In looking upon Him, the desire after our long lost likeness to God was to be awakened. That hope and faith which gave us courage to yield ourselves to be renewed after that image was begotten. To accomplish this, there was a twofold work He had to do. The one was *to reveal in His life the likeness of God,* so that we might know what a life in that likeness was and understand what it was we had to expect and accept from Him as our Redeemer. When He had done this, and shown us *the likeness of the life of God* in human form, He died that He might win for us, and impart to us, His own life as *the life of the likeness of God,* that in its power we might live in the likeness of what we had seen in Him. And when He ascended to heaven, it was to give us, in the Holy Spirit, the power of that life He had first set before us and then won to impart to us. the one depends on the other. For what as our Example He had in His life revealed, He as our Redeemer by His death purchased the power. His earthly life showed the path. His heavenly life gives the power in which we are to walk. What God has joined together no man may separate. Whoever does not stand in the full faith of the redemption, does not have the strength to follow the Example. And, whoever does not seek conformity to the image as the great object of the redemption, cannot fully enter into its power. Christ lived on earth that He might show forth *the image of God in His life.* He lives in heaven that we may show forth *the image of God in our lives.*

The Church of Christ has not always maintained the proper relationship of these two truths. In the Roman Catholic Church, the former of the two was placed in the foreground, and following Christ's example was forced on them with great earnestness. As the fruit of this, she can point to a large number of saints who, notwithstanding many errors and with admirable devotion, sought literally and entirely to bear the Master's image. But, to the great loss of earnest souls, the other half of the truth was neglected. Only they who in the power of Christ's death receive His life within them were believed to be able to imitate His life as set before them.

The Protestant Churches owe their origin to the revival of the second truth. The truth of God's pardoning and quickening grace took its true place to the great comfort and joy of thousands of anxious souls. And yet, the danger of one-sidedness was not entirely avoided. The doctrine that Christ lived on earth, not only to die for our redemption, but to show us how we were to live, did not receive sufficient prominence. While no orthodox church will deny that Christ is our Example, *the absolute necessity* of following the example of His life is not preached with the same distinctness as that of trusting the atonement of His death. Great pains are taken, and that most justly, to lead men to accept the merits of His death. As great pains are not taken, and this is what is not right, to lead men to accept the imitation of His life as the one mark and test of true discipleship.

It is hardly necessary to point out what influence the way this truth is presented will exercise in the life of the Church. If atonement and pardon are everything, and the life in His likeness something secondary, it follows as a matter of course that the chief attention will be directed to the former. Pardon and peace will be the great objects of desire. With these attained, there will be a tendency to rest content. If, on the other hand, conformity to the image of God's Son is the chief object, and the atonement the means to secure this end as the fulfillment of God's purpose in creation, then, in all the preaching of repentance and pardon, the true aim will always be kept in the foreground. Faith in Jesus and conformity to His character will be regarded as inseparable. Such a

Church will produce true followers of the Lord.

In this respect, the Protestant Churches still need to go on to perfection. Only then will the Church put on her beautiful garments, and truly shine in the light of God's glory—when these two truths are held in that wondrous unity in which they appear in the life of Christ Himself. *In all He suffered for us, He left us an example* that we should follow in His footsteps. As the banner of the cross is lifted high, *the atonement of the cross* and *the fellowship of the cross* must equally be preached as the condition of true discipleship.

It is remarkable how distinctly this comes out in the teaching of the blessed Master Himself. In fact, in speaking of the cross, He gives its fellowship more prominence than its atonement. How often He told the disciples that they must bear it with Him and like Him. Only thus could they be disciples, and share in the blessings His cross-bearing was to win. When Peter rebuked Him as He spoke of His being crucified, He did not argue as to the need of the cross in the salvation of men. He simply insisted on its being borne, because to Him as to us the death of self is the only path to the life of God. The disciple must be as the Master. He spoke of it as the instrument of self-sacrifice, the mark and the means of giving up our own life to the death, the only path for the entrance into the new divine life He came to bring. It is not only I who must die, He said, but you, too. The cross, the spirit of daily self-sacrifice, is to be the badge of your allegiance to Me. How well Peter learned the lesson we see in his Epistle. Both the remarkable passages in which he speaks of the Savior suffering for us—"Christ also suffered *for us*...who His own self bare our sins in His own body on the tree"; "He suffered for sins, the just *for the unjust*"—are brought in almost incidentally in connection with our suffering like Him (1 Peter 2:21,24; 3:18). He tells us that, as we gaze upon the Crucified One, we are not only to think of the cross as the path in which Christ found His way to glory, but as that in which each of us is to follow Him.

The same thought comes out with great prominence in the writings of the Apostle Paul. In one Epistle, that to the Galatians, we find four passages in which the power of the cross is set forth. In one we have one of the most striking expressions of the blessed truth of substitution and atonement: "Being made *a curse for us:* for it is written, Cursed is every one that hangeth on a tree" (Galatians 3:13). This is indeed one of the foundation stones on which the faith of the Church and the Christian rests. But a house needs more than foundation stones. And so we find that no less than three times in the Epistle the fellowship of the cross, as a personal experience, is spoken of as the secret of the Christian life. "I am crucified with Christ" (Galatians 2:20). "They that are Christ's have crucified the flesh with the affections and lusts" (Galatians 5:24). "God forbid that I should glory, save in the cross of our Lord Jesus Christ, by whom the world is crucified unto me, and I unto the world" (Galatians 6:14).

That Christ bore the cross for us is not all. It is only the beginning of His work. It opens the way to the full exhibition of what the cross can do as we are taken up into a lifelong fellowship with Him the Crucified One. And, in our daily life, we experience and prove what it is to be crucified to the world. And yet, how many earnest and eloquent sermons have been preached on glorying in the cross of Christ, in which Christ's dying on the cross for us has been expounded, but our dying with Him, in which Paul so gloried, has been forgotten!

The Church does indeed need to have this second truth sounded out as clearly as the first. Christians need to understand that bearing the cross does not, in the first place, refer to the trials which we call crosses. Instead, it refers to that daily giving up of life, of dying to self, which must mark us as much as it did Jesus, which we need in times of prosperity almost more than in adversity, and without which the fullness of the blessing of the cross cannot be disclosed to us. It is the cross, not only as exhibited on Calvary, but as gloried in on account of its crucifying us—its spirit breathing through all our life and actions—that will be the path to victory, to glory, and the power of God for the salvation of men, both to the Christian and the Church as it was to Christ.

The redemption of the cross consists of two parts—Christ bearing the cross; Christ's crucifixion for us, as our atonement, the opening up of the way of life: and our crucifixion, our bearing the cross with Christ, as our sanctification, our walking in the path of conformity to His blessed likeness. Christ the Surety and Christ the Example must equally be preached.

But, it will not be sufficient that these two truths be set forth as separate doctrines. They can exercise their full power only as their inner unity is found in the deeper truth of Christ our Head. We see how union with the Lord Jesus is the root in which the power of both the Surety and the Example has its life. We can also see how the one Savior makes us partakers both of the atonement and the fellowship of His cross. As we see both of these, we will understand how wonderful their harmony is, and how indispensable both are to the welfare of the Church. We will see that as it is Jesus who opened up the way to heaven *as much by the footsteps He left us to tread in as by the atonement He gave us to trust in,* so it is the same Jesus who gives up pardon through His blood, and conformity to Himself through His Spirit. And, we will understand how, for both, faith is the only possible path. The life power of this atonement comes through faith alone; the life power of the example no less so. Our evangelical Protestantism cannot fulfill its mission until the grand, central truth of *salvation by faith alone* has been fully applied, not only to justification, but to sanctification, too. That is, to the conformity to the likeness of Jesus.

The preacher who, in this matter, desires to lead his people in the path of entire conformity to the Savior's likeness, will find a very wide field opened up to him. The Christlike life is like a tree in which we distinguish the *fruit*, the *root*, and the *stem* that connects the two. As in individual effort, so in the public ministry, *the fruit* will probably attract attention first. The words of Christ, "Do as I have done" (John 13:15), and the frequent exhortations in the Epistles to love, forgive, and forbear even as Christ did, first lead to a comparison of the actual life of Christians with His. Then, they lead to the unfolding and setting up of that only rule and standard of conduct which the Savior's example is meant to supply. The need of taking time and looking distinctly at each of the traits of that wonderful Portrait will be awakened, so that some clear and exact impressions of what God actually would have us be can be obtained from it.

Believers must be brought to feel that the life of Christ is, in very deed, the law of their life, and that complete conformity to His example is what God expects of them. There may be a difference in measure between the sun shining in the heavens and a lamp lighting our home here on earth. Still, the light is the same in its nature, and in its little sphere the lamp may be doing its work as beautifully as the sun itself. The conscience of the Church must be educated to understand that the humility and self-denial of Jesus—His entire devotion to His Father's work and will, His ready obedience, His self-sacrificing love and kindly beneficence—are nothing more than what each believer is to consider his simple duty as well as his privilege to exhibit, too. There is not, as so many think, one standard for Christ and another for His people. No, as branches of the vine, as members of the body, as partakers of the same Spirit, we may and therefore must bear the image of the Elder Brother.

The main reason why this conformity to Jesus is so little seen, and in fact so little sought after among a large majority of Christians, is undoubtedly to be found in erroneous views as to our weaknesses, and what we may expect divine grace to work in us. Men have such strong faith in the power of sin, and so little faith in the power of grace, that they at once dismiss the thought of our being expected to be just as loving, just as forgiving, and just as devoted to the Father's glory as Jesus was. They think of it as an ideal far beyond our reach—beautiful indeed, but never to be realized. God cannot expect us to be or do what is so entirely beyond our power. They confidently point to their own failure in earnest attempts to curb temper and to live wholly for God as the proof that the thing cannot be.

It is only by the persistent preaching of Christ our Example, in all the fullness and glory of this blessed truth, that such unbelief can be overcome. Believers must be taught that God does not reap where He has not sown, that the fruit and the root are in perfect harmony. God expects us to strive and think and act exactly like Christ, because *the life that is in us is exactly the same as that which was in Him*. We have a life like His within us. What could be more natural than that the outward life should be like His, too?

Christ living in us is the root and strength of Christ's acting and speaking through us, shining out from us so as to be seen by the world.

It is the preaching of Christ our Example especially, *to be received by faith alone,* that will be needed to lead God's people on to what their Lord would have them be. The prevailing idea is that we have to believe in Jesus as our Atonement and our Savior, and then, under the influence of the strong motives of gratitude and consistency, to strive to imitate His example. But motives cannot supply the strength; the sense of utter inability remains. We are brought again under the law: we ought to, but cannot. These souls must be taught what it means *to believe in Christ their Example.* That is, to claim by faith His Example, His holy life, as part of the salvation He has prepared for them. They must be taught to believe that this Example is not a something, not even a someone outside of them, but the living Lord Himself—their very life, who will work in them what He first gave them to see in His earthly life. They must learn to believe that if they will submit themselves to Him, He will manifest Himself in them and their life-walk in a way surpassing all their thoughts. They must believe that *the Example of Jesus and the conformity to Him* is a part of that eternal life which came down from heaven, and *is freely given to everyone who believes.* It is because we are one with Christ, and abide in Him, because we have in us the same divine life He had, that we are expected to walk like Him.

The full insight into this truth, and the final acceptance of it, is no easy matter. Christians have become so accustomed to a life of continual stumbling and unfaithfulness, that the very thought of their being able, with at least such a measure of resemblance as the world must recognize, to show forth the likeness of Christ, has become strange to them. The preaching which will conquer their unbelief, and lead God's people to victory, must be brought to life by a joyous and triumphant faith. For it is only to faith—a faith larger and deeper than Christians ordinarily think necessary for salvation—that the power of Christ's Example taking possession of the whole life will be given. But, when Christ in His fullness, Christ as the law and the life of the believer, is preached, this deeper faith, penetrating to the very root of our oneness of life with Him, will come. With it, the power to manifest that life will also come.

The growth of this faith may, in different cases, vary much. To some, it may come in the course of quiet, persevering waiting upon God. To others, it may come as a sudden revelation, after seasons of effort, struggling, and failure; just one full sight of what Jesus as the Example really is, *Himself being and giving* all He claims. To some, it may come in solitude—where there is no one to help but the living God Himself alone. To others, it will be given, as it has been so often, in the communion of the saints. It is there, amid the enthusiasm and love which the fellowship of the Spirit creates, that hearts are melted, decision is strengthened, and faith is stirred to grasp what Jesus offers when He reveals and gives Himself to make us like Himself. But, in whatever way it comes, it will come when Christ, in the power of the Holy Spirit, is preached as God's revelation of what His children are to be. And believers will be led, in the deep consciousness of utter sinfulness and weakness, to yield themselves and their life as never before into the hands of an Almighty Savior. They need to realize in their experience the beautiful harmony between the apparently contradictory words: "In me (that is, in my flesh,) dwelleth no good thing"; and "I can do all things through Christ which strengtheneth me" (Romans 7:18; Philippians 4:13).

But root and fruit are ever connected by a stem, with its branches and leaves. In the life of Christ this was so, too. The connection between His hidden life rooted in God, and that life manifesting itself in the fruit of holy words and works, was maintained by His life of conscious and continual personal fellowship with the Father. In His waiting on the Father, to see and hear what He had to make known, in His yielding Himself to the leadings of the Spirit, in His submission to the teachings of the Word which He came to fulfill, in His watching unto prayer, and in His whole life of dependence and faith, Christ became our Example. He had so truly been made like unto us in all things, become one with us in the weakness of the flesh, that it was only thus that the life of the Father could be kept flowing freely into Him and manifesting itself in the works He did.

And just so, it will be with us. Our union to Jesus,

and His life in us, will most certainly secure a life like His. This not, however, in the way of an absolute necessity, as a blind force in nature works out its end. But instead, in the way of an intelligent, willing, loving co-operation—a continual coming and receiving from Him in the surrender of faith and prayer, a continual appropriating and exercising of what we receive in watchful obedience and earnest effort, a continual working because we know He works in us. The faith in the vitality and the energy of the life in which we are eternally rooted will not lead to sloth or carelessness. It will, as with Christ, rouse our energies to their highest power. It is the faith in the glorious possibilities that open up to us in Christ our life, that will lead to the cultivation of all that constitutes true personal fellowship and waiting upon God.

It is in these three points of similarity that the Christlike life must be known; our life like Christ's hidden *in God,* maintained like His in fellowship *with God,* will in its external manifestation be like His, a life *for God.* As believers begin to understand the truth—that we are indeed like Christ in the life we have in God through Him, we can be like Christ in keeping up and strengthening that life in fellowship with God, and that we will be like Christ in the fruits which such a life must bear—the name of followers of Christ, the imitation of Christ, will not be a profession but a reality. The world will know that the Father has indeed loved us as He loved the Son.

I venture to suggest to all ministers and Christians who may read this inquiry whether, in the teaching and the thought of the Church, we have sufficiently lifted up Christ as the divine Model and Pattern, in likeness to whom alone we can be restored to the image of God in which we were created. The more clearly the teachers of the Church realize the eternal ground on which a truth rests, its essential importance to other truths for securing their complete and healthy development, and the share it has in leading into the full enjoyment of that wonderful salvation God has prepared for us, the better will they be able to guide God's people into the blessed possession of that glorious life of high privilege and holy practice. This life will prepare them for becoming such a blessing to the world as God meant them to be. It is the one thing that the world needs in these latter days—men and women of Christlike lives, who prove that they are in the world as He was in the world, that the one object of their existence is nothing other than what was Christ's object: the glorifying of the Father and the saving of men.

One word more. Let us, above all, beware that, in the preaching and seeking of Christlikeness, that secret but deadly selfishness does not creep in. It leads men to seek Christlikeness for the sake of getting for themselves as much as is to be had, and because they would gladly be as eminent in grace and as high in the favor of God as they may be. God is love: the image of God is Godlike love. When Jesus said to His disciples: "Be ye therefore perfect, even as your Father which is in heaven is perfect" (Matthew 5:48), He told them that perfection was loving and blessing the unworthy. His very names tell us that all the other traits of Christlikeness must be subordinate to this one: seeking the will and glory of God in loving and saving men. He is Christ the Anointed: the Lord has anointed Him. For whom? For the brokenhearted and the captive; for those who are bound and those who mourn. He is Jesus—living and dying to save the lost.

There may be a great deal of Christian work with little of true holiness or of the Spirit of Christ. But, there can be no large measure of real Christlike holiness without a distinct giving up of oneself to make the salvation of sinners for the glory of God the object of our life. He gave Himself for us, that He might claim us for Himself, a peculiar people, zealous of good works. Himself for us, and us for Himself: It is an entire exchange, a perfect union, a complete identity in interest and purpose. Himself for us as Savior, us for Himself still as Savior; like Him and for Him to continue on earth the work He began.

Whether we preach the Christlike life in its deep, inner springs, where it has its origin in our oneness with Him in God, or in its growth and maintenance by a life of faith and prayer, of dependence and fellowship with the Father, or in its fruits of humility and holiness and love, let us always keep this in the foreground. The one chief mark and glory of Christ is that He lived and died and lives again for this one thing alone: *the will and the glory of the God of love in the salvation of sinners.* And to be Christlike means simply this: to seek the life and favor and Spirit of God only, that we may be entirely given up to the same object: *the will and the glory of the God of love in the salvation of sinners.*